S0-AHE-190

Writing at Century's End

Essays on Computer-Assisted Composition

Edited by

LISA GERRARD

UNIVERSITY OF CALIFORNIA, LOS ANGELES

Contributing Editors

JENNIFER BRADLEY

MICHAEL E. COHEN

ROBERT CULLEN

BARBARA ROCHE RICO

Random House   **New York**

221922

808.042
W9567

First Edition
987654321
Copyright © 1987 by Random House, Inc.

All rights reserved under International and Pan-American Copyright Conventions. No part of this book may be reproduced in any form or by any means, electronic or mechanical, including photocopying, without permission in writing from the publisher. All inquiries should be addressed to Random House, Inc., 201 East 50th Street, New York, N.Y. 10022. Published in the United States by Random House, Inc., and simultaneously in Canada by Random House of Canada Limited, Toronto.

Library of Congress Cataloging-in-Publication Data

Writing at century's end.

 Bibliography: p.
 Includes index.
 1. English language—Composition and exercises—
Study and teaching—Data processing.   2. English
language—Rhetoric—Study and teaching—Data processing.
3. Computer-assisted instruction.   4. Word processing.
I. Gerrard, Lisa.
PE1404.W6944   1986   808'.042'0285   86-24766
ISBN 0-394-35961-5

Manufactured in the United States of America

All essays are original to this volume, and are printed with the permission of the authors.

PREFACE

Almost all of the essays in this collection originated as presentations at the UCLA Conference on Computers and Writing, held in May 1985. The excitement generated by the participants at our conference, as at the increasing number of computer conferences springing up around the country, testifies to the vitality of this new field and the immediacy of the questions it raises. The contributors to this volume offer some answers and pose new questions. As writers, educational administrators, software developers, and instructors from grade school to college, they address a wide range of issues—from concrete, practical considerations (such as designing classroom exercises) to political and theoretical ones (such as the instructor's status as software developer and the limits of artificial intelligence).

Many people contributed to this volume. I would like to thank Richard Lanham, Carol Hartzog, and Lauren Cammack, who encouraged and supported the conference that gave rise to this collection, and the conference participants, whose inquiries, experiences, and enthusiasm inspired it. I am also grateful to Carol Dana Lanham, Mike Rose, and John Wright for helping me get started and for offering invaluable advice along the way, and to Steve Pensinger, Fred Burns, and the people at Random House for their expert help and commitment. To the contributing editors, Jennifer Bradley, Michael Cohen, Robert Cullen, and Barbara Roche Rico, I owe a special debt. Their patience, honesty, wisdom, and common sense saw the book to its conclusion and had everything to do with shaping the finished product.

Lisa Gerrard

CONTENTS

v

FOREWORD

One of the most powerful uses of the high-speed digital computer is to aid human problem solving. The technology offers the potential for a new synthesis between human and machine, one that can expand and even change the way people approach difficult and complex problems.

What led to my initial interest in computers was just such a capacity. Back in the "dark ages" of computing (the early 1970s), when the best that we could do was to connect a bunch of rickety old teletype terminals to a minicomputer and watch them chug away at 100 baud (11 characters per second), I turned to this technology to solve a difficult teaching problem. I was daily confronted by 600-odd biology students in a general biology class for majors at UC Berkeley. I realized that these students needed a chance to look upon science as discovery—to explore and investigate, to become part of the scientific endeavor. By simulating biological systems, the computer became their "laboratory," providing an environment where students could test hypotheses and perform experiments.

A by-product of this activity was my reluctant introduction to another of the computer's capacities, that of word processing. I shall not bore you with the usual testimonial about how using the word processor changed my life. I did, however, follow the oft-repeated progression from casual use to addiction—from using the computer as a glorified typewriter for final drafts, to complete dependence on the machine in all stages of the writing process. What interests me most is not that the computer acted as divine interceder in my acts of creation but that, in the process of the intercession, it had, I believe, a profound influence on my writing process itself.

For example, I used to be a firm believer in the detailed outline. Following sage advice provided by my graduate mentor, I would carefully think through every idea and organize it in the standard format, with each heading corresponding to a paragraph (or, if I were really ambitious, to a sentence) of final text. I would then produce a first draft, revise it, and write the second (and final) version. Done. Not so now. Now, I often come to the blank screen with an equally blank mind and wait for the inspiration to somehow flow out through my fingers. I let it come in a jumble, oblivious to sequence, structure, and the details of style or syntax. The whole piece then slowly shapes itself, through seemingly endless cycles of revision. All of this, of course, without my ever having heard of Peter Elbow! I have no idea whether my writing is *better* for this approach; I do not believe that it is quicker or easier to produce. What is clearly different, however, is my writing *process*. A new symbiosis has evolved.

The word processor that so captivated me was not even designed especially for English composition; it was more of a programmer's writing tool. Years later, while at UCLA, I began to wonder what would happen if there were a computerized writing environment that specifically addressed a writer's needs. Out of this curiosity, and out of my collaboration with Michael Cohen and Lisa Gerrard, grew the WANDAH project. WANDAH (an acronymn that cost me two days of intense effort and has since been abandoned in favor of the more neutral label HBJ Writer[1]) was consciously designed to provide tools for the beginning writer at *every* stage of the writing process. The **Prewriting** part of the program prompts freewriting, outlining, and invisible writing, whereas the **Word Processor** has features (like the split screen and OOPS key) that make revising easier and accidental catastrophic loss of the outpourings of one's brain less likely. The **Reviewing and Revising** portion of the program does some of the things that computers do best—word counts, spelling checks, pattern matching for oft-misused words and phrases. But it also helps the writer easily create an *ex post facto* outline from the text that can be useful in revealing structure (or lack thereof). And it makes peer review a great deal easier.

It's much too soon to know whether WANDAH and systems like it, created specifically to nourish the new symbiosis between the beginning writer and the computer, will meet with success. Will the new collaboration between people and machine increase creativity and productivity? Will a dependence arise that will ultimately benefit all those who are ensnared in its web? Or will something of value be lost? Just as the advent of written language reduced the need for (and the reward associated with) prodigious memory capacity, may dependence on computers for writing have an adverse effect on the final written word? I think not. But I believe we need to be aware of the changes that such systems are making, and will continue to make, in the writing process.

This book is directly concerned with these changes. It describes a variety of experiences using computers as composition aids, charting the effectiveness of the new technology in the writing classroom. Though some authors warn against making (or crediting) extravagant claims about computers, the preliminary consensus is that the technology offers power and potential.

No matter what the criticism, the computer is never going to go away. Those of us who are hooked will remain hooked, and our numbers will continue to increase. Software will continue to be developed to make the machine more useful. But only when we pay attention to how the computer is affecting our writing will we know whether we have made progress. This volume is a step in that direction.

Ruth Chervin Von Blum
VENICE, CALIFORNIA

---

[1] WANDAH was developed under a grant from the EXXON Education Foundation to UCLA. It is being distributed under the name *HBJ Writer* by Harcourt Brace Jovanovich, San Diego, California.

Writing at Century's End

Essays on
Computer-Assisted Composition

Introduction

LISA GERRARD

When word processors first appeared, writers quickly recognized their potential as creative tools rather than as transcribing aids. Originally designed for secretaries, to facilitate typing and formating business documents, word processors have enabled writers to revise as they transcribe and even to bypass transcription altogether, conceiving and shaping their work as they type. By allowing writers to copy, move, erase, insert, and endlessly adjust their text without retyping, word processors have encouraged experimentation and invited creativity. Of course, the quality of the finished text depends, as it always has, on what writers have to say and on their skill in saying it. But by reducing the mechanical awkwardness of revising, the computer has freed writers to think, and (to use Stephen Marcus's term) to rethink.

During the seventies, a handful of pioneers introduced word processing as an instructional tool for writing.[1] Since then, the computer, having made its way into most areas of our lives, has become a widely accepted component of the writing course. Word processing software has been supplemented with software (or "course-ware"—educational software) to help students in various stages of the writing process. Some programs ask questions to spark ideas, encourage spontaneous outpouring to relieve writer's block, and foster consideration of audience and purpose; others offer aids for outlining, organizing, and checking spelling, usage, punctuation, syntax, grammar, and even style.[2] In the past five years, instructors have experimented with these and other uses for the computer, exploring not only the new software but also the hardware technology as it has expanded, changed, become less expensive and more accessible, and offered new possibilities for writing instruction.

The first group of essays (Part One) describes some of these experiments. Edward M. Jennings has created "paperless" writing classes, in which students and instructor communicate through an electronic bulletin board. Students use the computer to comment on each other's work-in-progress, while the instructor sends electronic mail to the whole class and to individual students. Don Payne finds that electronic mail extends his students' audience. In a pedagogy course, student teachers monitor the papers of students at several schools; and a technical writing class continues a project begun by another class during a previous term. Other instructors have drawn on the tools of the software industry. Erna Kelly's students collaborate on a project for writing and testing computer documentation; as they learn good

---

[1] Ellen Nold, "Fear and Loathing: The Humanist Approaches the Computer," *College Composition and Communication* 26 (October 1975). Hugh Burns, "Stimulating Rhetorical Invention in English Composition through Computer-Assisted Instruction," *ERIC Document 188 245* (1979).

[2] Ellen McDaniel, "A Bibliography of Text-Analysis and Writing-Instruction Software," *Journal of Advanced Composition*, forthcoming.

technical writing practices, they simultaneously explore the computer's potential for full-scale revising. Diane P. Balestri's classes learn about composing by writing computer programs; her students take a course in Pascal programming concurrently with English composition, applying to their writing the planning and design strategies of Pascal. Reaching beyond word processing, Elaine O. Lees has experimented with a Kurzweil Reading Machine—which transforms writing into sound—to get students to hear sentence errors they wouldn't catch by proofreading silently, reading aloud, or listening to someone else read their paper.

These innovations have changed writing instruction. John C. Thoms compares his computer-centered classroom to a one-room schoolhouse. Instruction is individualized, as students work at their own pace and on different pieces of software. Many of the authors have noticed a similar phenomenon: Given tools that encourage revising and that address their individual needs, many students are developing more self-confidence and control over their writing. Whether they work alone or collaborate with their peers, they are taking charge of the writing task rather than surrendering all power to the instructor. The evolution of this attitude has accompanied a change in the instructor's role. As several authors point out, the instructor in the computer-based writing class is often a coach rather than an authority, an advisor rather than an expert. For the most part, this change has benefited instruction. The electronic classroom is a friendly, informal place; camaraderie among students increases (Jennings); students help each other (Kelly), though, as Payne observes, competition remains; and students are more motivated (Thoms).

Benefits accrue in the writing as well. Valarie Meliotes Arms discusses how the computer fosters creativity, especially among writers with visual imaginations. By enabling engineering students to move around large chunks of text, the computer makes writing a nonlinear, spatial process. Ease of revision invites all kinds of writers to play with text and to be receptive to new ideas and flexible about changing old ones—important components of creativity. By facilitating revision, the computer also teaches, more tangibly than ever before, that good writing almost always requires rewriting. So too, as Jennings and Payne have found, the computer can teach students to write for an audience; with electronic mail, they are writing for real, responsive readers. These authors are optimistic about what the technology can offer us; the computer not only enhances writing instruction but also transforms it.

At the same time, the computer, like most innovations, has introduced problems. Computer-based courses with a nonauthoritarian structure do not work equally well for all students. Such is the conclusion Andrea W. Herrmann draws from her experiment with a course serving students whose social backgrounds, academic skills, and learning styles differed greatly. Some students thrived on the go-at-your-own-pace structure, others felt overwhelmed by it, and a third group just "got by." The computer alone could not erase the differences that make some students self-motivated learners and others dependent on outside authority. Herrmann argues that the way we integrate computers into our courses must take into account such differences in learning style.

The second group of essays (Part Two) expands this critical look at computer-based writing. David N. Dobrin and John E. Thiesmeyer consider limitations in the technology. Dobrin argues that idea processors are not what they purport to be—they inhibit, rather than encourage, creativity. Though idea processors can help writers who work from a detailed, linear outline, they restrict the free range of ideas preliminary to most writing. Like Dobrin, Thiesmeyer faults the software industry for misrepresentation. He finds that artificial-intelligence programs do not replicate human reasoning, as some manufacturers claim, but check for only the most superficial features of a text. Unable to analyze textual content or complex semantic structures, and imperfect in what they do analyze, such programs have limited use in composition instruction.

While instructors assess the hardware and software offered from the outside, they confront a tangle of social and political problems *within* academia. One of the most pressing issues is evaluation. As administrators pay for computer equipment and the support to go with it, how can we justify the cost? Michael E. Cohen explores the expectations and assumptions that govern how we evaluate the computer's effect on student writing and argues that evaluators must narrowly define what they are looking for. He suggests that attempts to assess an overall improvement or degeneration in students' writing will fail because neither statistical data nor impressionistic evidence can accurately measure writing quality. As Deborah H. Holdstein explains, even if we do satisfactorily document the computer's value, we still confront a variety of other political issues: What incentives lie ahead for instructors who lavish time and imagination on software development and curriculum redesign? Will their creativity be rewarded or viewed as a detour from traditional research and publication, the conventional route to tenure? Furthermore, the humanist who works with computers develops a whole new network of relationships, many of which cause conflict: contention within the department over what software to buy, interdepartmental competition for access to hardware and software, miscommunication with programmers and technical assistants, disagreement with the university over ownership rights for software development. Clearly, computers have changed the instructor's position outside the classroom as well as within it.

These essays suggest that what may seem a simple writing tool may in fact change our teaching, our students, our status, and our profession in unexpected ways. To maintain some control over these changes, we need to pay attention to our assumptions about computers—what they can do, what goals they should support, who uses them and how—and to the social and psychological implications of our work. In the final essay, Stephen Marcus argues for such consideration. Humanists who bring computers into the profession must not succumb to "thinker's block" but must instead look closely at several key issues. Are we pressuring our students into "computer literacy," giving them as much anxiety as opportunity? Is our computer curriculum conditioned by stereotypes based on race, gender, or socioeconomic status? Do we understand what we are doing and why we are doing it well enough to survive a possible backlash against computers in education? By confronting these questions, we can help put the technology to its best use now and prepare ourselves for what is to come.

Marcus's thesis—that we need to consider carefully how computers affect our work—is the thread connecting all the essays in this volume, as each author reflects on his or her experience with the technology. If the overall tone is optimistic, it is because computers are enhancing what is already a dynamic time for writing instruction. Just as research into writing processes is changing the way we teach writing, so computers are reinforcing much of this research and offering new applications for its findings. Many instructors committed to a product-oriented pedagogy, for example, have found that word processing simplifies the composing–revising cycle to such an extent that it sometimes obliterates the boundary between writing and rewriting. Several participants in the UCLA conference commented that this discovery converted them to a process-centered approach. Computers can, in fact, advance composition research itself. Researchers studying writing processes may want to look at what writers do when working with a tool that *invites* textual change. And their study can benefit from the computer's capacity to record and store key presses, keeping track of writers' actions as they work. [3]

The computer's flexibility is cause for optimism. As a multipurpose tool, the computer can support widely differing pedagogical applications: from the traditional (tutoring grammar) to the exploratory (writing without paper, responding without paper or voice, and receiving evaluation and criticism from a machine). The varied uses instructors have found for this tool testifies both to their imagination and to the computer's versatility. Furthermore, the computer has not just changed what we do in the classroom. It has also influenced our role there and our status as humanists. These influences may well be constructive. Certainly the computer has made us less parochial, having moved us outside the traditional confines of our expertise and into the engineering, business, and computer science departments. This timely move coincides with writing-across-the-curriculum projects and efforts to make academic writing approximate "real-world" writing. As technical departments get increasingly concerned about writing and humanities departments get increasingly interested in computers, we have an opportunity to communicate—even to collaborate—with professionals across campus.

As we consider these possibilities, we also need to think about our own values and assumptions. Computer-based composition, like all technology, is not neutral or value-free. It reflects our beliefs and assumptions about what constitutes good writing instruction (grammar tutorials? process-based programs?) and about who should use the computers. Where budgets are limited, do we favor basic writers,

---

[3] For an example of this kind of research, see the following studies on how a word processor affects the composing processes of different writers: Lillian Bridwell, Parker Johnson, and Stephen Brehe, "Composing and Computers: Case Studies of Experienced Writers," in *Writing in Real Time: Modelling Production Processes*, ed. Ann Matsuhashi (Norwood, N.J.: Ablex, in press); and Lillian Bridwell, Geoffrey Sirc, and Robert Brooke, "Revising and Computing: Case Studies of Student Writers" in *The Acquisition of Written Language: Revision and Response*, ed. Sarah Freedman (Norwood, N.J.: Ablex, in press). See also Mark P. Haselkorn and Robert J. Connors, "Computer Analysis of the Composing Process," in *Computers and Composition: Proceedings of the Conference on Computers in Writing: New Directions in Teaching and Research*, ed. Lillian S. Bridwell and Donald Ross (Houghton, Mich.: Michigan Technological University, 1984), pp. 139–158; and Sandra J. Balkema, "Studying the Composing Activities of Experienced Computer Writers," in *Computers and Composition: Proceedings of the Conference on Computers in Writing: New Directions in Teaching and Research*, ed. Lillian S. Bridwell and Donald Ross (Houghton, Mich.: Michigan Technological University, 1984), pp. 23–35.

who may need the extra help, or technical writers, who need computer experience? What impact will the computer have on populations that differ in age, social class, income, ethnicity, gender, academic standing, and course of study? Do all these groups have or need equal access?

Particularly troublesome is the myth that computers will teach composition for us, an idea welcomed by those who would prefer to teach something else (usually literature) and decried by those contemplating their own obsolescence. The computer is an unusually capable tool, but it can't even begin to do what a human does. An instructor who reads a draft is aware of the complexities of its context: She interprets it in terms of the reading, research, discussion, and personal experience that generated it. She can intuit what the beginning writer meant but couldn't say; she engages in a dialogue with him to elicit ideas and information that help them both understand what the paper is, or might be, about. She responds not just to the paper as an artifact but also to the person who wrote it, drawing on the age, sex, personality, and what she knows of the interests and cultural background of the writer.

In short, what makes writing instruction human is what makes it effective, and no computer, no matter how friendly, can replace a human teacher. We must caution against instructors who expect to park their students in front of machines and go off to pursue their own research. Against administrators who would trade the tutoring center for a computer lab. Against an increase in class size based on the mistaken belief that computers lighten the teaching load. Such actions (and I know of instances of all of them) miss the point. Computers offer us new techniques for doing what we have always done—assigning and responding to writing and *writers*—but they cannot do our work for us and should not be expected to.

Furthermore, computers have not reduced the work load of any instructor I know but have more often added to it. Now we inspect new software, write modified instruction manuals, tend to machinery, coordinate lab schedules, and construct new assignments, new curricula, and even our own software. As most of the writers in this volume testify, this work has paid off in more effective and enthusiastic learning. At the same time, our efforts have put us in a position to determine what direction computer-based composition will take. Like the contributors to this collection, we may not always agree on the benefits of computer-assisted composition or on the solutions to its problems, but as computer users, software developers, and curriculum designers, we can decide what these benefits and solutions will be. This is both a responsibility and an opportunity.

PART ONE

PEDAGOGICAL ISSUES

Paperless Writing
Boundary Conditions and Their Implications

EDWARD M. JENNINGS

What happens when writers don't use paper? In the spring of 1985 I conducted an advanced writing course using a central computer, time-sharing terminals, and an electronic bulletin board. Before we began, I imagined all sorts of good things we might try to do. Along the way, the replacement of ink and paper with electronic dots produced some surprises. Looking back at what did happen in the paperless environment, I'm willing to declare that writing instruction, and the ways in which we evaluate its success, will change even faster and more radically than we have expected.

THE SETTING

We took advantage of three opportunities supported by the central DEC-20 computer. The full-screen EMACS editor functioned as a word processor. Students could write, revise, and edit without retyping to accommodate their changes. The "bulletin board," a storage place dedicated to our class inside the DEC, was where students "posted" assignments after composing them at their own work spaces. Everyone could read (but not alter) the posted pieces that accumulated on the bulletin board. Finally, there was a mail-message system known as MM through which I could address an individual or the whole class and they could send me notes. We all used it for sending each other comments about posted pieces. The notes were sent electronically to each person's "mailbox," where they waited for the addressee to log in on the DEC.

The course itself is somewhat unusual. As in other writing courses in our department, only the grades Satisfactory and Unsatisfactory are assigned. Unlike other courses, however, its province is nonacademic writing. Called "Practical Writing," its purpose is to help undergraduates practice somewhat more "generic" skills than many college classes call for. We often try to simulate "real-world" rhetorical conditions with our assignments, but we usually avoid such highly specialized genres as the business letter.

The course has always attracted more students than we can enroll in its dozen sections. A few who signed up for this high-tech section, knowing they would have to use the scary computer, did so because they wanted any section of any writing class at any price, and I suspect a few seniors wanted it because an S/U class would be a soft spot in their last semester. Most were competent but uncoached writers, from all over the university, who were willing to practice hard.

The students wrote at terminals in Computing Center or dormitory user rooms. They submitted their assignments each week by sending them from their work space to the bulletin board. I used a terminal to read their posted work and returned comments to them through the mail-message system. The writers could read everything on the bulletin board and could send each other comments. They could arrange to print a copy of a draft to work on away from the terminal, but no papers were passed to other people. Once a week we met, almost socially, to talk over how things had been going and what we would work on next.

At our first meeting I handed out rudimentary instructions about how to approach a computer for the first time and about how to use the word processing program. The writing students competed with computer science students for time at the terminals. Only one participant was already an expert with the DEC; she helped us solve problems that arose in using the machine. Everyone else experienced some degree of frustration with "the system," but none regretted struggling through it.

Many components of the writing and teaching processes remained familiar in the novel environment. Although word processing made some writing chores easier, I don't think the technology had dramatic effects on how students went through the stages of composing. A couple of them reported shifting from drafting at home with pencil and paper to doing all their composing at the terminal, but few others had much to say about their personal writing process.

READING AND RESPONDING TO THE SCREEN

Having to respond at the terminal to what I read on its screen did change my own habits, however. I had known that I wouldn't be able to scribble red hieroglyphics in margins, but that didn't bother me. I had looked forward to having my copy editor's hand restrained, because I wanted to concentrate on responding to ideas and commenting on coherence and cohesion.

So I began the semester by calling up each piece on the screen with the word processor. Sometimes they were still in draft form, which gave me opportunities to work with writing that the student didn't think of as finished. I was able to insert long notes between lines, write extended responses to ideas, ask questions about locutions that confused me, even compose sample alternative paragraphs. The editor provided space that margins had never offered. When I returned the piece to the student's work space, she could make changes easily and delete my interlineations.

As my wishes of many years came true, however, they turned out to be as unfulfilling as the ones in fairy tales. I just couldn't resist the temptation to spend too long writing too much about too many "errors." More important, I realized that I had fallen into a trap halfway between copy editing to correct surface errors and responding as a reader to a fellow writer's efforts; I was trying to get the students to turn their texts into what I would want them to look like if *I* had written them. The on-line editor did let me do what I had always wished there had been room on the papers to do, but I began to wonder whether doing so was a good idea.

Before long I settled into a different routine. After signing on my terminal, I read a piece from the bulletin board. Then I hopped to the mail system and sent the writer a note. Because that hop meant letting the text I had just read slip off the screen into electronic limbo, so that I could use the screen for writing the note, I had to rely on memory and an occasional penciled reminder as I composed my note to the writer. At first, while I was stumbling toward this routine, I was frustrated; I kept wishing I had those annotated pages beside me to glance at as I commented. Then I found myself remembering better and recalling differently. I learned to read in order to grasp and respond to what the writer had actually said. I almost stopped translating her text into what I thought she was trying to say, and I found that my comments, composed from the jumble of immediate recollection, came to reflect what an interested reader remembered best about what the writer had accomplished.

My conscience nagged me from time to time as this regimen evolved. I was not helping the students learn to avoid surface errors. I was not providing the ritualistic abstractions about clarity and organization and fuzzy diction that they and I were accustomed to. The notes I sent weren't even "holistic"; "impressionistic" is probably closer to the mark. As the group gathered momentum during the semester, however, I realized that I was treating people as writers instead of as youthful offenders.

What seemed at first to be a technological constraint, the disappearance of the text I was writing about, turned into a psychological release. Off screen, the text seemed far away. I treated it as finished and turned to the future. My response focused on accomplishment and on what I sensed the writer might want to try the next time. The writer interpreted my response as either praise or faint praise, and—lacking a scarred paper to refer to—could carry away from the episode one message aimed forward at the *next* piece, instead of backward at a rehash of what she had completed and said good-bye to.

WORKSHOPPING

The electronic bulletin board was supposed to widen the audience for the writers, and it did, but not exactly as I had anticipated. The intended model was a writers' workshop, in which papers are distributed in advance and every participant in the circle responds to everyone else's piece of writing.

I expected the bulletin board to smooth out the logistical problems surrounding advance distribution of papers, reduce the reluctance some people have about reading aloud, and eliminate the need to congregate on a schedule. Using the computer, writers could read and respond at whatever hour they wanted to look for a terminal.

But my experience had been in graduate workshops with a few people meeting 3 hours a week. When I asked the 20 paperless writers to read their classmates' work and to write to them what they thought about it, nothing seemed to go right. The timing was wrong: Readers working on their own schedules sometimes found what they'd looked forward to reading had not been posted by the time they wanted to examine it. Most important, the numbers were too large; I realized belatedly that I was asking them to read and write responses to 19 papers as well as to work on their own writing.

There were other differences between workshopping in a classroom and trying to do it electronically. The comments went straight from one reader to one writer instead of being "broadcast" to the whole circle. (Although I had imagined doing so, I did not try to have all the comments posted; there would have been 400 messages to plow through each week, 4 times as many as in a class of 10.) There were no voice inflections and no body language to interpret. Furthermore, the writers knew that I would be making a "professional" comment about each text; I surmise that knowing this diminished in their minds the importance of *their* responses.

Like other frustrations, however, these faded as the semester went on. In the first place, a large chunk of the benefit of workshopping occurred automatically when all the pieces were "published" on the bulletin board each week. The writers read what was up there and knew that their peers could read their work. The importance of the commenting procedure itself shrank in my eyes as I recognized that an awareness of an audience larger than one instructor was built into the technology. In the second place, I heard enough comments about "wanting to see what so-and-so did" and about "hoping so-and-so will tell me what he thinks of my piece" to know that those who wanted to "workshop" did so.

Although workshopping with the bulletin board did not work the way I had anticipated, I think it promoted what I had hoped for. By enlarging and dispersing the readership, and by inviting others to join in reading everything, the bulletin board encouraged writers to work through their own process of developing discrimination.

I suppose the reinforcement process went something like this: Student A liked B's and C's work, but after a glance ignored D. Writer B tried to imitate C and D but felt superior to A. Student C wanted to impress A and D (perhaps for reasons unrelated to writing) and knew that B was out of her league. This is a rather crude hypothetical model, but I believe it parallels the way students perceived and evaluated each other's work. And I am happy to imagine that the contrived reality of the bulletin board's audience, with its opportunities for nurturing taste and discrimination, benefited the students more than any amount of my professional wisdom alone would have.

ELECTRONIC CONFERENCES

The mail-message system, called MM, snuck up on me. I had planned to have the students use it for sending each other all those comments, but that didn't work. Instead of writing interlinear comments, I used MM to send observations to writers about their texts. And the system turned out to offer both a pseudo-classroom and a perpetual conference network.

The classroom component is obvious: I could broadcast a message about an assignment or about a prewriting exercise or an organizing technique that seemed generally pertinent. I could "lecture," in a sense. But I didn't know just when each writer would arrive at a terminal and read his mail; I didn't have everyone in front of me as I "talked."

The timing of sending and receiving is part of the peculiarity of electronic mail. Sending messages is as easy as telephoning: You dial and talk; no envelope, no delay. In some ways it's like sending a note. You have to compose coherently, because there's no one "listening" who can help straighten out misunderstandings as they arise. On the other end, the addressee treats a note in the in-box either like a call, replying while the incoming message is still on the screen (there's no need to look up an address) or like a note: file it and forget it. As sender, you know the addressee will get the message, but you don't know when or what he'll do about it. As recipient, you can pretty much do what you like about the message, including promising yourself to try to find it in the files later.

Because delivery is guaranteed, because it stays in the files, and because it is composed rather than uttered, a message sent by MM is substantial. But, because it exists only on the screen (or in a storage place only the recipient can scrounge through), and because the sender doesn't keep track of every message composed, a note sent by MM is ephemeral.

It is so much easier to send notes than to arrange appointments that the system becomes a perpetual conference. The "meetings" aren't at all like "see me in my office" conferences, however. There are no face-to-face smiles or acquiescent nods, no pugnacity or shoulder shrugging. There's no scheduling, no pressure to arrange equal time; the students get all the attention they ask for (but seldom much more). Either a writer or the instructor can initiate a "conversation" at any time, but neither party knows how soon the other will reply—or even whether there will be a reply. One student sent me a note almost every time she sat down at a terminal, but two or three students sent me no queries or responses all semester. My notes triggered some changes in posted texts, but there are no messages on file acknowledging my guidance.

INTEGRATED WRITING TASKS

The first few tasks paralleled some I had assigned in paper-bound sections in other years: some autobiography, a review of a performance, an entertaining introduction to a subject the writer felt experienced with. It was in working with these early pieces that I learned to change my strategy for commenting. But I had looked forward to using the technology as the basis for a truly "practical" task, one in which the writers could be as good at evaluating their performance as I could be. As the semester went on, I found several ways to integrate the technology, the writing tasks, and the workshop-like modes of evaluation.

The first system-reflexive task was to prepare some "how-to-do-it" documentation of the DEC itself. In some ways this was just another "instructions" assignment. Here, however, I found the ritual transformed into reality. The rhetorical situation had purpose, audience, and authoritative voice built in. The students had before them an example, my own attempt to show the uninitiated how to get started. Their task was to improve my documentation or expand it to cover a part of the operation I had not explained.

In writing documentation, the "student" is the authority, the genuinely transactive writer. The task calls for clear thinking about the precise extent of the reader's ignorance. The success of the documentation depends on how well it works: Can a real reader follow the instructions?

The technology and the task of explaining how to use it reinforced each other more powerfully than I had anticipated. All three parts of the encoding–decoding triangle had to be reconciled: The sequence of the sender's experience had to be recalled; the subject's dynamic, once grasped, had to be conveyed; and the receiver's processing of the information had to be accommodated. The task needed no artificial ground rules in order to encompass important transferable skills. Not everyone wrote perfect documentation, but I had enough inquiries and testimony to feel confident that most of the writers had grappled with the rhetorical dilemmas built into the assignment.

The documentation exercise guaranteed authenticity of rhetorical situation, but it was rather dry. I stumbled onto another task, a pair of pieces just as tightly tied to the technology, more fun, and comparably demanding, though in some ways less authentic. In the first week, the writers learned to play an old-fashioned computer game and had to explain what they thought were the best strategies for winning. The second week's assignment encouraged using the bulletin board for help in revising.

The game was an old chestnut called "Hammurabi." A player responds to choices presented on the screen as he runs a nation for ten years, making decisions about buying and selling land, about how much to feed the population, and about planting the fields. Each "year" the computer decides and reports how bountiful or skimpy the harvest was, how many people died, and how much grain is left in storage for food and seed. The player can calculate what the best choices will be in order to survive through all ten years, but he has to play the game a few times in order to figure out what needs calculating. The player–monarch usually gets lynched a few times before learning how best to connect the interdependent variables.

This "research project" was identical for all of the writers. All the materials were on the screen. Audience and purpose were the same for all. For the first deadline, the students gave the task their best shot but did not post their text. Then we all put our explanations on the bulletin board and went to work on the second part of the assignment, improving on the first version's technical accuracy and its readability. Most of the revisions also either eliminated excess introduction or supplemented the cryptic background information of the first version.

This pair of assignments required students to explore an unfamiliar subject, puzzle their way toward an optimal solution to the rhetorical challenge, and write a piece that looked better than the others on the bulletin board. Revising called for comparing one's solution to those of others, making judgments about quality, and rewriting to meet one's own complex standards of satisfaction.

TRANSFERRING AUTHORITY

As the semester went along, I was especially conscious of who really controlled what got written. Two previous experiences, and a suspicion they had planted, formed the background for my interest. Several years ago, a mature student kept asking me whether this sentence or that paragraph was satisfactory; I kept asking him if he'd thought about one or another alternative. He almost quit the course. But he analyzed his frustration and later reported that he'd been expecting me to tell him what was correct. We concluded that all his previous writing instruction had implied that there was one and only one proper way to say anything, that teachers knew what that way was, and that it was the teacher's job to provide the correct phrasing.

Another student revealed a similar assumption, although he never realized that he held it: One learns to write better by taking more writing classes. One has only to follow instructions; there is no other way to improve.

From these experiences and from subsequent observations, I began to suspect that most students are conditioned to "know" that "perfect" writing is a mystery and that they must depend on their instructors to initiate them into a realm beyond.

Because I consider this belief erroneous, I look for ways to diminish my authority and transfer responsibility for writing to the writer. So I was especially conscious of how the technology of paperless writing affected authority–responsibility relationships.

Eliminating paper eliminated the need to hand in and hand back student work and thus altered the implicit authority structure of our meetings. "They" were not required to "submit" in public, and the teacher-in-charge didn't have to hand down rewards and punishments to the seated congregation. The technology wiped out some of the lock-step uniformity that accompanies paper.

Responding to texts that had disappeared from the screen kept me from "correcting" papers. I could suggest that writers look at what other people had written; I could point out places where voice or audience or purpose had seemed shaky or inconsistent; but the emphasis seemed to fall on how the writer might think about approaching the *next* piece. The writers getting my comments did not have to prove they had followed instructions or even acknowledge receipt; they had independent control over communication. There wasn't much chance that a student would become dependent on me for more than interest, encouragement, and an occasional question or suggestion.

The writers were aware that the bulletin board expanded their audience. They all got at least a few messages about their texts from other writers besides me. Sharing their work also expanded students' comparative reference base. They could look to see what others had done and feel proud or ashamed (probably both) of their efforts. The process of judging for themselves presumably affected their personal standards and aspirations.

I observed that the MM system let writers initiate conferences whenever they felt like it; again, they had as much control over communication as I did.

Some writing tasks let the students be as expert as the instructor; they could estimate their own "success" against both pragmatic standards ("Does it work?") and normative standards ("How does it compare to my peers' work?") instead of those of a superior authority.

All of these circumstances are built into the technology. They transfer "power" to the writer, yet they don't seem to diminish respect for the instructor's experience or his ability to share it.

CONFRONTATION

Before the semester began, I had not wondered about how the students and I would meet and talk. My speculations had centered on how we would deal with the texts. I have already summarized a few of the ways in which the MM system seemed to pass some control of our relationship to the individual writers, but I should also illustrate what I take to be the positive implications of something that *didn't* happen.

Students didn't come to me after class, or at conference time, to quibble over the words I had inscribed on their pieces of paper. I didn't have to defend myself on a moment's notice. I probably would not have noticed the absence of those occasional embarrassing incidents if I hadn't been caught in an inconsistency.

A student found a comment from me in his MM in-box and sent a note asking, "What are you talking about?" When I called the text back to the screen to check, I couldn't figure out how I had seen in it what I seemed to have said I had. Without stopping to think, I sent back another note about what I thought after reading the text again.

Only later on did I wonder how I might have handled his question if he had had to carry the paper to my office. Would I have felt trapped and compromised? Would I have bafflegabbed the inconsistency away, complimenting him on his astuteness and demonstrating that I had really meant what I should have said? Would I have felt my infallibility threatened? Would I have apologized?

As I looked back on the incident, I realized that I had always accepted occasional confrontations with students as part of the job and that I had learned how to defend my authority gracefully, turning the incidents into no-lose conversations.

Inside the paperless writing environment, however, with its expanded audience and realignments of authority, getting "caught" in an inconsistency didn't constitute a conflict. I had no qualms about acknowledging (implicitly, with no explanation) that the same reader notices different things in a text on different readings. Thoughts of defending myself didn't occur to me until I looked back and saw what hadn't happened.

BOUNDARY CONDITIONS

Gravity is a boundary condition. The speed of sound once looked like one. So, for humans, are water and oxygen. They set outside limits on what can and cannot happen. Paper used to be a boundary condition for writing.

Seymour Papert, former codirector of the Artificial Intelligence Laboratory at M.I.T., once pointed out that teaching mathematics used to be controlled by pencil and paper (*The Computer Age* 76). There was no choice. The limits of the teaching process weren't set by either the nature of the subject or the way people learn. Whether it was old math or new math, every variation in what was taught or how the teaching was done had to operate inside the boundary conditions set by paper and pencil.

Now that we don't have to use paper in order to write, we can look analytically at what paper has forced us to assume and prevented us from doing. We are in the position of that imaginary person trying to build a house of cards. What happens when she turns off the gravity? The first few projects produce funny-looking houses and some questions about the several ways, not all of them recognized before, in which gravity influences house building.

Although I liked the looks of the first structure we erected in the paperless environment, I cannot assess whether the project was "successful." Customary ways to measure "success" are as paper-bound as our theories of coaching and teaching. Although I strongly suspect that impressionistic commenting, opportunities to read others' work and to write for an expanded audience, and increased control over discussions of texts ought to help students become better writers, I cannot demonstrate that the altered environment actually does shift authority and responsibility in the ways I suspect it does or that such a shift is necessarily good for undergraduate writers.

We will have to find different ways to assess our efforts—ways that acknowledge what the new technology can accomplish—because some variant of paperless writing will be everywhere within two generations. (The avalanche has begun and will reach campuses eventually. Strictly paper-bound classes will someday be rare, like courses in advanced Latin.) I suspect that interest in definitions and measurements of "good writing" and in methods for stimulating proper processes will diminish. We'll probably try to figure out how to arrange environments that nurture authority and confidence and discrimination and standards of self-satisfaction.

The transition will be gradual. At the beginning, we'll adapt the new scribal technology to do traditional jobs like correcting papers faster, drilling classes in useful processes, and printing better-looking papers. Eventually, though, we'll realize (after a struggle) that some of the old jobs don't need doing.

Meanwhile, there will have been a series of projects designed to examine sophisticated versions of our crude paperless experiment. From them, sooner or later, will come theory and practice and evaluation criteria that will amalgamate all the discoveries that await those who venture across the paper boundaries.

REFERENCES

Papert, Seymour A. "Computers and Learning." In *The Computer Age: A Twenty-Year View*, edited by Michael L. Dertouzos and Joel Moses. Cambridge, Mass.: M.I.T., 1980.

ACKNOWLEDGMENT

Warm thanks to Isabel Nirenberg, Kelly Kreiger, and Barry Leibson of Albany's Computing Center for all their help.

Edward M. Jennings
STATE UNIVERSITY OF NEW YORK AT ALBANY

Computer-Extended Audiences for Student Writers
Some Theoretical and Practical Implications

DON PAYNE

Prior to radio, television, and other modern forms of electronic communication, writing distinguished itself from speech partly in its ability to reach audiences remote in time and space. Now, with computers, writing can reach these extended audiences and still retain some of the rhetorical immediacy of spoken communication. Although the technology may be new, the complex speaking–writing issues associated with extended audiences can be traced back to classical rhetoric—back, for instance, to Plato. In *Phaedrus* Socrates complains that writing extends audiences too much. "Once a thing is put in writing," he says, "the composition . . . drifts all over the place, getting into the hands not only of those who understand it, but equally of those who have no business with it; it doesn't know how to address the right people, and not address the wrong. And when it is ill-treated and unfairly abused it always needs its parent [by which he means speech] to come to its help, being unable to defend or help itself." Socrates points out other advantages of speech over writing, too:

> Anyone who leaves behind him a written manual, . . . on the supposition that such writing will provide something reliable and permanent, must be exceedingly simple-minded. . . . [W]ritten words . . . seem to talk to you as though they were intelligent, but if you ask them anything about what they say, from a desire to be instructed, they go on telling you just the same thing forever.[1]

For Socrates, speech was dynamic; writing was static and thus inferior. (The computer, of course, has something to say about that distinction.) Longinus, in *On the Sublime*, comes to a different conclusion by recognizing the power of the extended audience as an imagined posterity. With speech we can extend the audience into the past, with writing into both past and future:

> It's well that we ourselves also, when elaborating anything which requires lofty expression and elevated conception, should shape some idea in our minds as to how perchance Homer would have said this very thing, or how it would have been raised to the sublime by Plato or Demosthenes or by the historian Thucydides. . . . A greater incentive still will be supplied if you add the question, "In what spirit will each succeeding age listen to me who have written this?" But if one shrink from the very

---

[1] Plato, *The Collected Dialogues*, trans. R. Hackworth, ed. Edith Hamilton and Huntington Cairns (Princeton: Princeton University Press, 1961), p. 521.

thought of uttering aught that may transcend the term of his own life and time, the conception of his mind must necessarily be incomplete, blind, and as it were untimely born.[2]

Socrates and Longinus illustrate the mixed blessing of writing's permanence. The shift from speech to writing, from sound to the alphabet was the first, and arguably the most basic, of many changes in the communication media, of which the computer is merely the most recent. It is perhaps impossible to talk about this concept without mentioning the name of Marshall McLuhan. Even though McLuhan's concepts have been the source of much controversy and are for many historically tainted by the events of the sixties and seventies, they can focus our attention in several useful ways.[3]

The very fact that professional journals and conferences are examining computers' effects on writing and on the teaching of writing implies that the medium— if it is not *the* message—is at least an important part of the message that we want to convey to our students. You may recall how McLuhan traces the technologies of communication through four major periods: the acoustic period of preliterate societies (where communication is predominantly oral and aural), the manuscript period (where writing begins to assert the visual sense and to anesthetize the aural), the typographic period (where the eye amputates the other senses), and the electronic period (wherein meaning is communicated to and generated by the central nervous system, as though bypassing the senses altogether). The stages of McLuhan's communication history are merely stages of emphasis; the new technologies never supplant the old entirely. Even as each rises to dominate, all the other modes still exist as communication choices. In fact, when we talk about writing and computers, we're not talking about an old process confronting a new medium but rather about an old medium facing a reincarnation into a new one.

McLuhan's views on electronic technology revive the speaking–writing issues posed by Socrates. McLuhan predicted that the age of electronic communication would return us to the oral base of preliterate society. We're all too familiar with some of the negative ways in which this prediction has come true. In recent public lectures, I have heard (the verb here being doubly ironic) a litany of studies and statistics lamenting the number of people in our society whose access to information is limited to the ear alone. I'm referring to such speakers as Jonathan Kozol describing illiteracy (a forced dependency on spoken communication) and James Kinneavy describing aliteracy (a self-imposed dependency on spoken communication, specifically the growing preference for visual over print journalism). And we all have heard writing teachers, perhaps even ourselves, observe that students would rather talk than write—even that they talk with greater facility than they write.

On the positive side, to return to a preliterate society is to restore to the language its natural communicative power. We can describe that power in various ways. It is the emphatic quality of face-to-face communication, the immediacy and

---

[2] Longinus, *On the Sublime*, trans. W. Rhys Roberts (Cambridge, England: Cambridge University Press, 1935), p. 83.

[3] The McLuhan concepts discussed here can be found primarily in *The Gutenberg Galaxy: The Making of Typographic Man* (Toronto: University of Toronto Press, 1962); *Understanding Media* (New York: McGraw-Hill, 1964); and *The Medium Is the Massage* (New York: Random House, 1967).

vitality of a spontaneous rhetorical situation, the energy of a dialogue unfolding meaning before us, or the truth-seeking capacity that Socrates attributed to dialectic. In part, the psychological and sociological concerns of oral language are reflected in the recent emphasis on a process approach to the teaching of writing, specifically in such activities as freewriting, brainstorming, talk–write rehearsals of ideas, and peer evaluation. We may argue whether computers are merely exposing the writing process or are in fact reshaping it, but we should agree that there's a certain serendipity about computers happening into our profession just when process questions and models are so much on our minds. Some future McLuhan may even look back on the computer's relationship to process-centered theories of composing as one of cause and effect.

Computers are leading many researchers to reexamine the writing process. Developing an intelligent computer tutorial system, for example, means taking a new look at how the tutoring process works, how a teacher communicates a particular skill to a student through that direct, face-to-face contact that we now want to emulate electronically. One goal of simulations, tutorials, and even drill-and-practice programs is to capture the computer's capacity to sequence and freeze time. We want to reproduce that special moment when two minds share in discovering meaning, whether that fresh association be stimulated by bits of information stored in human memory or bits of data stored in electronic memory.

McLuhan's words for this meaning-making moment was "simultaneity." He saw us leaving behind a typographic age (characterized by linearity and rationality—that is to say, meaning by measured reflection, not meaning by spontaneous generation) for an electronic one. McLuhan recognized that electronics collapses the temporal and spatial delimiters between the event and its significance. Dan Rather calls the outcome of an election before all the voters have cast their ballots; a local television reporter comments on an event's significance while that event is still unfolding behind her. In such cases, we might long for a return to the clear separation between the event and its analysis. But when the event is a piece of student writing and the analysis is our evaluation of that writing, the greater our distance from the process itself (and hence from the writer), the more difficult we find it to diagnose, to advise, to instruct. We have come to realize how incomplete a picture the product alone gives us; we want to be closer to the writing event.

As we think of computers and writing, McLuhan's idea of simultaneity has paradoxical results. Time and space are narrowed and compressed; audiences and contents are extended and expanded. Let's look at some of the implications of this paradox.

The time–space compression turns writers into publishers. After all, microcomputers have given new life to the term *cottage industry*: There is now even an Association for Electronic Cottagers. At the simplest level, the writer needs only to press a print function on a keyboard to "publish." The low-cost laser printer brings us even closer to realizing the effect that McLuhan saw in xerography:

> If book and hardware sales need to be large to defray expenses, electronic publishing by Xerox can dispense with large-scale publics and markets almost entirely. Even more easily than by hand-press, a writer can publish a few copies of his work for his friends

by simply multiplying the typescript. In fact, Xerox completes the work of the type-writer. A poet composing at the typewriter is "publishing" his work, as it were, while composing. Xerox gives to that fact a new meaning."[4]

Intriguingly, this merging of writing and publishing can potentially generate readers where there were none before. This may sound like some sort of electronic alchemy or microchip magic—and perhaps it is—but I'm simply talking about drawing readers into the writing process at what formerly would have been a prepublication stage. Again and again I've seen the "published" look of computer print-outs or of neat phosphor-formed letters work its reader magic. It seems either to give the writer enough confidence to ask a nearby person for a reader response or to create enough curiosity in a bystander to volunteer as a reader. I've had strangers stop to read over my shoulder while I was composing on my portable computer, staying on to engage in a discussion of both my text and my composing process. Conversely, I've gone to the microcomputer lab in my department at Iowa State University to do some computer work and ended up collaborating with a colleague on some document freshly "published" on a video display screen or on fanfold paper. I've often watched a class of college or high school students composing at microcomputers or terminals and have seen how that high-pitched, machine-gun assault of the printhead on paper can draw teacher or classmate to see what's been produced, to read, to linger in discussion. There would seem to be no reason why pad-and-pencil groups couldn't do the same thing, of course, but to some degree computers have socialized writing, making the private more public in the process. Writers can now join painters as people who share their art not only as the thing-made but also as the thing-in-the-making, substituting as the conspicuous tools of their craft their portable micros for an easel, canvas, and paints.

For students, one practical effect of writer-as-publisher can be the extension of audience to readers other than teachers or classmates, the extension from proximate readers to remote ones. How does this benefit students? For one thing, remote audiences mean a more realistic writing context than that provided by either the immediate but captive classroom audience or Longinus's vague future audience. Students can now attempt larger, more meaningful writing tasks because these need not be completed in a single course or semester. In my business and technical editing course, computers have made it easier to use real campus and community projects. Word processing and magnetic storage have overcome scheduling prob-lems by enabling students to do parts of a project, the rest to be completed by students enrolled in subsequent semesters. Such assignments approximate the record-keeping and management problems of long-term projects, simulate realistic communication to audiences within an organization, and demonstrate the collab-orative nature of much transactional writing. At the same time, the class that continues the project does not need to start from scratch or to waste valuable time retyping text. In short, we approach the continuing communication context out of which real writing is generated. Even the old pen-pal writing has been updated by

[4] Marshall McLuhan, "At the Moment of Sputnik the Planet Became a Global Theater in Which There Are No Spectators But Only Actors," *Journal of Communication* 24 (1974): 49.

computer networks, and class newsletters are becoming highly professional floppy-disk publications distributed to readers inexpensively just by mailing a disk from one school to another.

Computers can also extend the traditional composition classroom by linking classes at different schools through modem and telephone line. Mona Smith, a high school English teacher, and I are currently working on just such a project, funded by the Northwest Area Foundation. In my teacher education classes, I emphasize the benefits of teaching writing-as-process (rather than writing-as-product), but ironically I've been unable to capture for my students the dynamics, or (to use McLuhan's word) the "simultaneity," of writing. The troubling question is this: How can my student teachers value "process" when I can show them only "products" divorced from the living students who created them? The computer, of course, poses an electronic solution to the logistics of bringing together a university methods course and a high school writing course. For a state like Iowa, the possibility of interactive instruction linking the many small junior and senior high schools with the major universities is attractive. With that in mind we set out to see how practical it would be to use microcomputers between two institutions, given the inevitable equipment and scheduling problems.

Essentially, our project went like this. A sophomore paragraphing workshop at the high school was taught in the usual way, except that students wrote their assignments at school on Apple IIe microcomputers. The texts of these assignments were sent, via modem and phone line, to university students in a senior-level course on the teaching of writing in secondary schools. Each student teacher was assigned to read and evaluate the writing of two or three high school students. We hoped that this mini-class arrangement would aid the teachers' transition to full-class practice teaching and improve writer–reader rapport. Ideally, we wanted the student teachers to experience the fragility and complexity of the student–teacher, writer–evaluator relationship, to develop realistic expectations of student writing, and to become accountable writers themselves by sharing their work with high school students. For the high school sophomores, on the other hand, we saw possibilities for benefits in three areas. Assuming that word processors offer a set of procedures more complete and systematic than those usually practiced by beginning writers, we wondered whether computer-based writing would provide models for revising and editing. We further wondered whether the writer–publisher compression would boost the students' self-image by making it easier to go from initial ideas to printed copy. We also expected readers beyond the composition classroom to provide more of the questions, suggestions, and encouraging comments that growing writers need. For all the students involved, we expected a more reasonable view of computers as practical, nonthreatening tools for writing. Finally, on a larger scale, we hoped to achieve greater curricular continuity between the university and the high school involved and to establish a model for cooperation that other schools might adapt to their writing programs.

Our project is still under way, but we've already had some pleasant surprises. For one thing, the students complained on the days that they couldn't spend class in the microcomputer lab. It is hard for us to imagine these same students complaining about being denied a full class period for in-class writing; yet their lab time was spent entirely on writing and rewriting. During each of those sessions the students composed with quiet intensity.

One other unexpected result has seemed to be a greater quantity of writing. Not only did the high school students spend more time actually writing; they also wrote more in the time allotted. Their writing workshop usually focuses on paragraph-length assignments, but the computer speeded up the mechanics of the writing process to the point where the students began writing longer essays. Similarly, in the composition methods course, the student teachers typically devoted more time to evaluating writing than they had in the past. In fact, both high school and university students have asked that the project be expanded to allow for more frequent exchanges of writing, especially of revised assignments. It's refreshing to have students ask for more work. To this extent, at least, our predictions about the motivational benefits of an extended audience for student writing seem to have been accurate.

In projects like this, computers help create extended audiences in three senses. They extend them quantitatively by simply creating more readers for student writing; they extend them rhetorically by introducing readers whose interests, knowledge, and demands pose new tasks for the writer; and they extend them reciprocally by making available interactive readers whose feedback can initiate new cycles of writing and responding. In this way, computers help us catch meaning in the making and bring some of the dark machinery of composing into the light of the video screen. Perhaps they even answer some of Socrates's complaints about writing as unyielding text.

Computers do seem to hybridize the processes they touch—private thinking and public communicating, drafting and publishing, inventing and editing. My own electronic drafts appear visually before my eyes as a new species: part outline, part interlinear translation, part half-formed notes, part musings, part check list. The implications of such hybrid forms are not altogether clear. For example, the two groups of high school students who participated in our project showed marked differences in prewriting habits. Those not using the computer did little prewriting at the beginning of the course, considerable prewriting by the end. Those using the computer developed no clear prewriting stage at all. Are concepts like "prewriting" and "drafts" incompatible with a single, fluid, evolving electronic text? Will the organization of longer writings suffer from lack of prewriting? Can too much "simultaneity" lull writers into accepting looser structures of discourse? If we can foresee some benefits of extended audiences, we ought to be ready to count our losses, too. Whenever we extend one of our senses through a new technology, McLuhan suggests, we run the risk of amputating another. Perhaps our challenge as educators is once again to map out the golden mean as we attempt to define the role of computers in the teaching of writing.

Processing Words and Writing Instructions

Revising and Testing Word Processing Instructions in an Advanced Technical Writing Class

ERNA KELLY

When asked how word processing influences the composing process, writing teachers often point out that computers encourage risk taking at all stages of the composing process—prewriting, drafting, reviewing, revising. This risk taking seems to be a result of two related computer features: the ease of revision that computers provide and the screen display of these revisions. As Stephen Marcus points out, students no longer feel their writing is set in stone. Words moving across the screen, scrolling up and down, and appearing and disappearing show students how fluid writing can become (157–158).

In the prewriting and drafting stages, risk taking can help students capture the ideas that might have been lost in premature editing. It can also help students write more fluid prose. On the other hand, the use of the computer sometimes causes prose to become loose and unstructured, either stylistically or organizationally. One teacher, Charles Moran, notes that word processing has made his style "breezier," closer to spoken language. This, as he sees it, is neither a loss nor a gain. His earlier style suited some situations; his new style fits others. If purpose and audience require it, he finds it easy, given the computer's revision capabilities, to tighten his new, looser style (115). But will Moran's students revise as he does? How much will students who compose at a word processor actually revise? And what kinds of revisions will they make? Will they fix only typographical and mechanical problems? Or will they go further to make stylistic revisions? How many students will take even greater risks and make global revisions, revisions that involve restructuring the whole paper or large sections of it?

Theoretically, computers should encourage students to make global revisions, the kinds of revisions teachers often have difficulty eliciting from them. The ease with which students using word processing can add, delete, and rearrange large sections of text should make students more willing to move beyond mechanical and stylistic changes and to take greater risks in their revising. However, Richard Collier speaks for many when he observes that his students did not revise globally; instead they continued to concentrate on surface revision, much as they had before they began using computers (149–155).

Perhaps students find it difficult to move to global revisions on their own because, as novice writers, they cannot re-see their texts. It is certainly difficult to rethink a paper no matter how it is produced. Yet perhaps the ease with which a student can change spelling, punctuation, words, and phrases on a computer exacerbates the problem. By spending time prettying up the text, a student can delude herself into thinking she has truly revised it. Lillian Bridwell, Paula Nancarrow, and Donald Ross note that spelling checks, punctuation programs, and the like can cause some students to produce "manipulated" rather than revised text. They also warn that revising or manipulating only one screen at a time may introduce coherence problems as well (383).

Weaning students from surface revision is one of the most important issues that computer-assisted writing classes face. Some teachers suggest that intervention—a student–teacher conference, for example, or a peer review session at an intermediate stage of the writing process—might help students learn to revise globally (Daiute, 143; Pufahl, 91–93; Schwartz, 49). Students must see a need for global revision before they can or will use the computer's revising capacities fully.

The suggested remedy of intervening at an intermediate stage is a good one that will work with any assignment. However, there is an assignment that can encourage a wide range of revision strategies without requiring teacher intervention: writing and testing a set of directions. This assignment has an additional benefit: It prepares students for writing in the work place.

OBJECTIVES

I teach an advanced seminar in technical writing. In designing the course, I knew I wanted students to work with the kind of writing they were likely to encounter after they graduated. I also wanted students to understand, through practice, how much of writing is actually rewriting. An assignment that called for students to use a computer while writing and revising instructions, I felt, would help me meet both goals.

In addition to meeting students' long-term goals, I wanted the course design to respond to the students' interests. Some of my students planned to work as writers in industry or government. They might be asked to help draft instruction manuals for a new product. Or they might be assigned to revise a personnel manual. They might draft government documents that contained directions: a loan application, for example, or a tax form. Those who did not plan to become professional or technical writers would also frequently encounter instructions in the work place. For example, the accountant or engineer who became a manager might find herself writing directions for her subordinates. And even if she never drafted directions herself, learning how to develop a good set of instructions would make her a better judge of instructions used in her company or division. For those who did not plan to work in industry or government, writing instructions could still prove useful. Several other students in the class planned careers in academia, biology, or psychology. The biologists were graduate students already supervising undergraduate labs. If not now, then very soon, they would need to write lab instructions for students working under them. And one of the psychology majors was already writing instructions for the editorial board of a student-run research journal when he joined the class.

In addition to encountering instructions in the work place, these students would also use computers. This factor, as well as the general outcry over the inadequacy of computer manuals, helped me to refine the project further. Students would use computers for all stages of this project, and they would write instructions for using computers in word processing. I chose word processing because it would be accessible to everyone in the class and because it would be the most common computer application these students would encounter in their work.

I wanted to introduce my students to as many of the advantages of word processing as possible. I especially wanted them to experience the advantages the computer offers the writer who makes global revisions. Any type of writing assignment would lead them to discover the computer's capabilities for making surface revisions quickly and simply. A letter would do. (In fact, many word processing manuals have learners write and revise a short letter for just this purpose.) However, not all assignments help students discover the advantages of using a computer for global revision. Writing and testing instructions can accomplish this goal.

Writing and testing instructions also make students more aware of their audiences. The assignment helps students understand how punctuation, diction, metaphor, layout, organization, and repetition can affect their audience; it shows students how readers use directions. Even more important, the project helps students discover the challenge of writing one document for multiple audiences—very important knowledge for them to carry into their work. The same report, for example, might be read by experts in engineering, in accounting, and in transportation. Memoranda go to superiors as well as to subordinates.

Finally, a secondary goal of this project was to encourage collaboration. This project required a good deal of class interaction, which gave the class a sense of group identity and encouraged students to help each other with the remaining assignments. This interaction foreshadowed the collaboration they would encounter in the work place, but it also helped create an atmosphere very conducive to the teaching of writing.

THE PROJECT

My inspiration came from several sources: an article by William Van Pelt in *Educational Computing* (38–39), a project at the University of Minnesota (Winkler *et al.*, 1–15) and the Document Design Center's research on effective written instruction (Redish, 1–8; and Goswami *et al.*). In Van Pelt's class, students (mostly computer science and science majors) wrote different instructions for several audiences: hardware specialists, programmers, and beginning software users, for example. The University of Minnesota group wrote instructions for beginners at a word processor. My class would write for an audience with a basic, but not a sophisticated, knowledge of word processing.

For the project's target, I chose the school-supported word processing system, "PC-Write," simply because it was what we had at hand. Students would work with the "PC-Write" manual (Wallace, Version 2.1). In reviewing the manual, they saw problems in its format, found the instructions sometimes unclear, and deemed the indexing inadequate. Still, the "PC-Write" manual is better than many manuals, especially in tone and pace: It simply left room for us to work.

Because the students were not word processing experts (some were beginners) and because we had a limited amount of time, I decided that, rather than writing instructions from scratch, they would rewrite difficult sections of the manual. I allotted almost half of the semester (7 weeks) to the project. Even so, we had time to revise only 8 out of a possible 23 sections of the manual. An instructor who had taught "PC-Write" to his students and a consultant for Academic Computing Services (ACS) helped me determine which sections my class would revise. I chose sections that had posed difficulties for learners and yet taught features that were frequently needed. ACS was helpful in pointing out which sections had drawn the most complaints from the university at large and which ones even ACS consultants had found difficult. My class revised sections on moving and marking text; using the split screen; centering, transposing, and underlining; creating footnotes; formating the left margin; the find-and-replace feature; the hard-space, soft-hyphen, and form feed characters; and the ruler file.

The project itself was divided into several stages: (1) gaining familiarity with word processing, (2) designing instructions, and (3) testing and revising.

During the first stage, I taught the class just enough word processing to enable them to produce a piece of writing: They learned to create, edit, save, and print a file; to set margins; and to reformat paragraphs. They also chose (from my list) the feature they would revise and learned how to use that feature. This step fostered collaboration. I encouraged them to work in pairs and to go beyond the manual's instructions, considering friends, relatives, and the ACS consultants as resources (as sources of information that would help them to learn the features they had selected). Many followed this advice. In addition to fostering collaboration, learning the assigned feature also increased the students' audience awareness. Reading the manual's instructions without my help made students more aware of how instructions anticipated (or failed to anticipate) their needs as learners.

The project's second stage focused on the principles of effective document design. At this stage, students needed to define their purposes and audiences clearly: They identified their purpose and audience on an index card and handed it in for my approval. They then created a task list; that is, they divided the instructions for their features into learning tasks. During this segment of the project, we also discussed characteristics that make instructions easier to follow—for example, the Document Design Center's finding that headings are more effective when couched as "questions, statements, or verb phrases" than when couched as "single nouns or noun strings" (Redish, 5). This research, along with the students' definition of their audience and creation of a task list, increased the students' audience-awareness. Once they were aware of what would help an audience move through a lesson easily, the students, collaborating in pairs, revised their sections of the manual.

The third stage involved recursive testing and revising. Students first used protocol analysis. Each pair of students and I had a copy of their instructions. As students sat near me with their copies, pens, and paper, I sat at an IBM-PC terminal and read their instructions aloud, trying to use them as I read. We tape-recorded my reading—hesitations, misreadings, and all. They noted and recorded my actions, reactions, and facial expressions. I sometimes skipped sections of text, re-reread sections, or hit the wrong keys. I groaned and laughed alternately. Sometimes I must have looked anxious, especially when I found myself unable to move forward in a lesson. Protocol analysis completed, the students revised their drafts, trying to eliminate the problems I had encountered. After revising these drafts, they prepared to test them again, this time against a control group using the original version from the manual. Subjects for the test group and the control group came from the class itself, from the English Department, and from a freshman composition class. All subjects had only a basic knowledge of "PC-Write." The test I helped my students devise consisted of a time test and a questionnaire. The time test sought to discover whether their version took less time to complete than the original version, one sign of increased effectiveness. The questionnaire was designed to discover whether the subject could complete the lesson being tested, whether the instructions were clear, and, if not, at what points they became unclear. Using the questionnaire and time test, students tested the twice-revised version against the original. Finally, they wrote test reports that summarized their findings and made recommendations based on these findings. They submitted their test reports and the two versions of their lesson to me. (I already had copies of the original "PC-Write" versions.)

Like the other stages, this stage (especially the protocol analysis) alerted students to how an audience responded to their writing. But most important, students learned how successful revision requires an awareness of one's audience. From my facial expressions, gestures, and mistakes during protocol analysis, students could see where they needed to clarify their directions. The effects of successful revision were reinforced by the success the test subjects had in using the twice-revised sections. In addition to gains in audience-awareness and revising ability, the students' familiarity with computers and computer manuals grew as they moved through each of the stages.

It is true that my students could have completed an instruction-writing assignment without computers. They would have learned how to write and judge instructions as well as how to collaborate. They would also have had lessons in revision. However, they would have missed the chance to become familiar with word processing and to use a computer manual. True, writing instructions without the computer would have made students see the need for global revision. But the computer's ability to banish much of the tedium from reproducing the text after each stage of revision made multiple revisions not only possible but even welcome. This, I hoped, would encourage students to push revising to the limit, reinforcing the notion and practice of global revision more deeply than would have been possible without the computer.

ASSESSMENT

To assess the effectiveness of the project, I used the students' test reports and both versions of their lessons. I also used the informal verbal feedback I received throughout the project—in class, after class, and during office hours. Finally, I designed a questionnaire for the students to answer anonymously at the end of the project and used their responses in my assessment.

The test reports showed that the students' revisions had been effective. Overall, more subjects completed the new versions than the original "PC-Write" versions of the instructions. Subjects also found the newer instructions clearer than the old. The time taken by subjects able to complete the lessons in the old and new versions was about the same; thus the revised versions did not decrease the time needed to learn a feature. This finding, though, can be explained by revisions the students made. For example, although the manual includes some practice sections, many students incorporated additional self-tests both to reassure the user and to prevent the user from becoming completely lost. Students also wrote recaps at essential points within the lesson. Even though these features demanded more user time, the revised lessons seldom took longer to complete than the original versions. Only in one instance was the time increase significant: It took subjects 63 minutes to complete the new mark-and-move section but only 35.5 minutes to complete the old version. The new centering, transposing, and underlining section took an average of 11 minutes to complete; the old, 9.4 minutes. On the other hand, the new find-and-replace version took only 4 minutes to complete as opposed to 17 minutes for the original version. For all the other sections, subjects took the same amount of time to complete both versions. The added features enabled more users to understand and complete the lessons.

Although some students suggested additional revisions, I did not ask them to revise any further. They had learned the steps necessary for similar projects in the work force; in a real situation, they could continue revising as long as necessary or as long as budget and time constraints allowed. Furthermore, because protocol analysis had revealed the greatest need for revision, most students found the revisions they would make at this point minor, compared with those they made right after protocol analysis.

Students' answers on my questionnaire showed that they felt the project had helped prepare them for writing in the work place. When asked how important the project was to their growth as technical/professional writers, the majority indicated that it was quite important. Many noted that the project had simulated a work situation more closely than anything they had written before and that it had introduced them to computers. When asked to rate the various steps in the project, students responded that testing, especially the protocol analysis, had taught them the most. This suggests that audience-awareness and revision based on this awareness figured prominently in their scheme of values. When asked what advice they would give to students about to begin this project, students answered, "Write as if your audience were morons" and "Write as if you were writing for a friend." On the other hand, they thought clarifying the goal and audience early was only "somewhat helpful." This response seems to undercut their other indications of audience-awareness. I suspect they did not understand the value of this step. I found that half the class needed to rewrite vague notions of goal and audience; had they not clarified these points, I doubt that the project would have been as successful as it was. Collaboration (working in pairs and consulting with friends and ACS staff) was rated second only to testing in importance. The questionnaire suggests that students perceived the goals I had set for the project as important and felt these goals had been met.

The questionnaire provided more than an assessment, however; some of the responses offered an opportunity to teach the students more about their audiences. Both questionnaire answers and informal verbal feedback called my attention to what the students termed the "overlap problem." Some of them had been assigned sections in the manual that depended on the user's understanding another fairly sophisticated feature. To create footnotes, for example, a user needs to know how to mark and move text. The students writing instructions for footnotes or other features that assumed special previous knowledge were creative: They learned the necessary feature(s) and wrote a mini-lesson within their own lesson. Because they had assumed that a user would read a manual from beginning to end, however, they felt their situation was artificial. Actually, studies of reading in the work place show that people dip into manuals for what they need to know. Often they do not even use the table of contents or an index. The students were no doubt correct in assuming that users with a complete manual could, for example, turn to the "Mark and Move Text" section when they discovered that they needed the ability to mark and move text in order to produce footnotes. Still, I'm not so sure that my students' mini-lessons were a bad thing. If users who wanted to produce footnotes for their manuscript were referred to a nine-page "Mark and Move" section, would they continue? I think the mini-lesson (much shorter than nine pages but sufficient for producing a footnote) incorporated in the larger lesson would be welcomed by many users. This overlap question not only alerted my students to reading habits in the work place; it also alerted them to the problem of writing one document for an audience whose members have different levels of experience, often a crucial problem in designing instructional materials.

The project's most important result, however, was the range of revision it elicited from students. In comparing the students' two versions (the revision of the original section of the manual and the revision of that revision) with the original, I found students had made a variety of adjustments. Contrary to frequent findings suggesting that many students make only surface revisions, these students' revisions covered a wide range. Certainly surface revisions are very important in writing instructions, and my students did change punctuation and words. In one lesson they fixed a comma splice; in another they changed passive voice to active. But they also reduced sections and reorganized large portions of their lessons. They divided material into smaller sections via layout. For example, they broke up paragraphs into numbered steps or into smaller sections with subheadings. They added sections: introductions, overviews, sample text for the user to type in, self-tests, and reminders at the lesson's end. And in one instance, students even changed an analogy to make the associations more positive. The original analogy, comparing the "hold" area in marking and moving text to a penalty box for hockey players, became a freezer holding gourmet food.

SUMMARY

Having students write and test instructions is an ideal way to ensure that they move beyond using word processing merely to make a text look pretty. Protocol analysis made the need for global as well as surface revision very clear to my students: If they did not make major, as well as minor, changes in their texts, users could not complete the tasks their texts were describing. Having a chance to compare the success of their revision with that of the original instruction via the text and control groups also added incentive.

Although some individuals occasionally became discouraged, the class's energy, enthusiasm, and involvement remained fairly high throughout the project. And in addition to learning a good deal about writing effective instructions, the class learned to use word processing effectively.

I would continue to teach word processing at the beginning of this project. Perhaps because so much else was demanded of them, students did not have much time to think about their initial fears (a number of students wrote on the questionnaire that they had overcome their fear of computers). By combining the writing and testing of instructions with word processing, the project showed students how much writing involves rewriting. One student told me that, in the past, she had always handed in papers knowing they needed more revision. She had felt she simply could not type them one more time. This was the first time she had not let anything she thought could be improved go unchanged.

Finally, the project gave my students a genuine sense of accomplishment. Academic Computing Services (ACS) asked for copies of the revised lessons. As a result, the students have a project to list on their resumés and some useful writing to put into their portfolios, and ACS has eight well-written and tested lessons.

REFERENCES

Bridwell, Lillian, Paula Nancarrow, and Donald Ross. "The Writing Process and the Writing Machine: Current Research on Word Processors Relevant to the Teaching of Composition." In *New Directions in Composition Research*, edited by Richard Beach and Lillian Bridwell. New York: Guilford Press, 1983.

Collier, Richard M. "The Word Processor and Revision Strategies," *College Composition and Communication* 34 (1983): 149–155.

Daiute, Colette. "The Computer as Stylus and Audience." *College Composition and Communication* 34 (1983): 134–145.

Goswami, Dixie *et al. Writing in the Professions.* Washington, D.C.: American Institutes for Research, 1981.

Marcus, Stephen. "Real-Time Gadgets with Feedback: Special Effects in Computer-Assisted Instruction." *The Writing Instructor* 2 (1983): 156–164.

Moran, Charles. "Word Processing and the Teaching of Writing." *English Journal* 72 (1983): 113–115.

Pufahl, John. Letter. *College Composition and Communication* 35 (1984): 91–93.

Redish, Janice. Director, Document Design Center, American Institutes for Research. "Using Cognitive Science in Developing Materials to Train Writers." Unpublished paper, 1983.

Schwartz, Mimi. "Computers and the Teaching of Writing." *Educational Technology* November 1982: 27–29.

Van Pelt, William. "Documentation—The Missing Link." *Educational Computing* October 1982: 38–39.

Wallace, Bob. *PC-Write*. Version 2.1. Computer software. Quicksoft, March 1984.

Winkler, Victoria *et al.* (Rhetoric Department, University of Minnesota). "Procedures for Designing and Evaluating Training Manuals." Unpublished paper, 1983.

Algorithms and Arguments
A Programming Metaphor for Composition

DIANE P. BALESTRI

Writers are now a significant group of computer users in the commercial market, and, as a result, teachers of composition have at their disposal an impressive array of good software for improving their students' writing. These include data base programs for organizing notes and ideas, word processing programs for drafting and revising text, and communications programs for sharing drafts with faculty and peers for comment and evaluation. We all know that students can learn about composing by *using* computer programs. I will argue here that students can also learn about composing by *writing* computer programs. The act of programming in an artificial language can be taught to students as an efficient and effective model for the much more complex act of composition and as a valuable metaphor for changing students' attitudes toward both the process and the product of their writing efforts. By bringing computing as an activity, rather than the computer as a tool, into the writing classroom, I am attempting to modify not the environment in which the act of writing takes place but, through analogy and analogous practice, the nature of that act itself.

There is a substantial debate currently under way among computer scientists about the value of teaching programming to more than the very few students for whom programming will be a profession. But if programming is to become an esoteric activity, rather than the basic skill we once thought it would be, how useful is it for composition teachers to look to programming as a prototypical writing activity? One provocative answer to that question comes from Seymour Papert, who has pointed out in his groundbreaking book, *MindStorms*, that teachers can use instruction in programming as a powerful vehicle for teaching critical thinking skills.[1] Papert also demonstrates that programming enthralls students when it is taught well. My own college-level students have not escaped this fascination. They willingly haunt the computer lab at night, driven by the need to write programs that *work right*; their all-nighters for English composition, I fear, are more often provoked by procrastination than by enthusiasm. As a composition teacher, I have been intrigued to discover what habits of thinking and writing are being so enthusiastically practiced in the late-night computer lab. How are they related to the habits of thinking and writing that I have been developing for those same students in my own composition classes? If these programming habits are good habits, how can I annex them to improve my students' composition skills? Is there value in that need, driven by machine re-

---

[1] Seymour Papert, *MindStorms* (New York: Basic Books, 1980).

jection, to make a program *work right,* and how can such a value be transferred?

These were some of my questions in the fall of 1982, when I began a year's sabbatical to explore the analogous relationship I thought might exist between writing computer programs and writing critical essays. I studied Pascal, largely on my own, read my way through the current theories of both programming and composition, and talked extensively with colleagues.[2] I gradually came to understand that the process of writing a well-structured program and the process of writing a well-structured essay are basically the same. More important, I saw that this new writing process that students acquire and practice with such energy as they learn structured programming can be systematically utilized in the composition classroom as a practical model for the process of prose compositions.[3]

Before any new model for an old task can be said to be "practical" for purposes of instruction, however, it must first capture the imagination of the students to whom it is presented. It must revolutionize their way of thinking about that task. It must indeed offer a new metaphor. In the case of composition, for instance, we learn what students already understand about their writing process by looking at the metaphors they use to describe it. We can then begin to improve their writing by replacing weak and faulty metaphors with strong metaphors that represent a better understanding of the writing process.

When my freshmen describe their work, the metaphors they naturally choose are those of a dock worker or a stock clerk: They speak of "filling up" the pages and "sticking in" the quotations. If you teach writing, are you not annually as depressed as I am by the inevitable freshman question, "Are we allowed to *put in* our own ideas?" When computer programmers describe their work, on the other hand, the metaphors they use are those of an architect: They speak of "designing" and "constructing" their programs.[4] This programming metaphor for writing as design and construction can suggest to students a new understanding of the writing process. It raises the prospect of an experience much more intellectually stimulating and rewarding than that suggested by their own implicit metaphors of manual labor.

I have brought this programming metaphor to my freshman composition classroom with the help of a grant from the Fund for the Improvement of Post-Secondary Education. So that the metaphor is not abstract, but is in fact part of their daily experience, I require that all my students be concurrently studying at an introductory level the programming language Pascal as taught by a computer scientist committed to good principles of structured programming, which I describe below.

[2] I am particularly grateful to Bryn Mawr colleagues Sandra Berwind and Jay Anderson and to Richard Walton of the University of Montana, who at the time was conducting a similar project with support from the Sloan Foundation.

[3] By "structured" programming I mean the methodology that has emerged along with very high-level programming languages in the past decade. Proponents of structured programming strategies advocate rigorous and logical analysis and organization of thought prior to coding. I describe some of their strategies here. A popular and easily read introduction to structured programming is *Pascal with Style: Programming Proverbs* by Henry Ledgard, Paul A. Nagin, and John F. Hueras (Rochelle Park, N.J.: Hayden Book Company, 1979). These authors, interestingly, attribute their inspiration to *Elements of Style* by William Strunk and E. B. White

[4] See, for example, E. W. Dijkstra, A *Discipline of Programming* (Englewood Cliffs, N.J.: Prentice-Hall, 1976); Kenneth Orr, *Structured Requirements Definition* (Topeka, Kansas: Ken Orr & Associates, 1981); David A. Higgins, *Program Design and Construction* (Englewood Cliffs, N.J.: Prentice-Hall, 1979).

The programming and composition courses are separate in meetings, assignments, grading, and credit, but we as the faculty worked together in planning the project and coordinating our materials.[5]

For my purposes, actual concurrent study of writing and programming is valuable for students but not essential. Any student who knows something about programming could benefit from this approach. In a different implementation of this cross-disciplinary approach to writing at the University of Montana, for instance, students took quarter-courses in computer programming and logic before taking English composition; this sequential arrangement seems to have worked as well as concurrent study.[6] It is essential, however, that programming be taught as a structured process. By "structured," my colleagues in computer science mean a process that in a reasonably well-planned and orderly way creates a well-designed and orderly product. In some programming languages, such as BASIC, it is possible to input machine code in an unstructured, line-by-line manner. This process of programming by accretion can lead to a product—a program—that, even if it works, is long, sloppy, and exceedingly difficult for a human reader to follow. The model I wish to offer my composition students is that of a planning and development process that leads to a fully conceived and executed piece of writing. In Pascal, the machine does not process code that is input line by line; it accepts only a full text, a complete design.

As the two courses in composition and programming proceed in parallel during September, relationships between the two kinds of writing being practiced emerge rapidly and quite naturally. Because my students are novice programmers in an introductory Pascal course, they produce very simple programs at first; only later do they encounter the methodology for developing complex, structured programs. Thus, before I can discuss the programming process as a metaphor for composition, I begin by pointing out basic characteristics of the program itself—the product—that make it a useful model for its counterpart, the composition. For instance, a program must be mechanically correct to be even minimally acceptable to the machine. The computer tolerates neither creativity nor sloppiness in syntax, spelling, or punctuation. Furthermore, that conventionality in written expression extends to the kinds of sentences that can be built and to the logical relationships that can be articulated among the sentences. Knowing the conventions of Pascal, and writing within those conventions, are fundamental and are rewarded. The accuracy necessary to write usable Pascal is, for my purposes, excessive; human readers of English are naturally more tolerant than machines of a range of usage, especially if the chosen range suits the topic. My students' early encounter with the fussiness of accurate programming, however, reveals to them the power of conventional usage to convey meaning. Thus punctuation and syntax articulate relationships among the elements of a sentence: The semicolon denotes a balance that the comma cannot represent; subordination creates hierarchies of significance. Attention to mechanical details helps to make an essay *work right*.

[5] My colleague was Jay Anderson, Director of Academic Computing at Bryn Mawr College. We shared in one another's classroom experience, and I must credit Jay with writing every essay I assigned during the semester. I did less well in writing his programs.

[6] Richard Walton, *Computer Programming and Expository Writing: The University of Montana Cooperative Composition Experiment* (unpublished).

A second and more important characteristic of the computer program is dynamism: A program that works accomplishes something. Typically a program begins with data, transforms those data, and yields new results. Output results from input but does not replicate it because transforming activities have intervened. Thus, in an early exercise, students write a program that transforms a length given in meters to the same length given in yards. In some sense, this is merely a descriptive program, which renames its original object in different terms. But how much more lively it is as a simple model than the circling September essays of my freshmen, in which the introduction is repeated in the body and summarized in the conclusion and nothing is actively reconsidered and freshly viewed in between!

Finally, the program represents the solution to a problem which has had to be defined and understood before the program could be written. Along with Linda Flower and inspired by her, I think writing is well taught as a problem-solving activity,[7] and in the computer program I have a vivid and compelling model for problem solving in my students' immediate experience. The model I draw on here is not the computer program that describes the elements of a mathematical procedure, such as the solution to a quadratic equation, but the program that requires students to engage a nonmathematical problem both imaginatively and systematically. A simple example occurs as they are introduced to the graphics capacity of the machine: How to write a program that prints out a ten-row triangle of asterisks? Students can easily write ten commands (one to describe each row), but analysis of the triangle-making activity leads them to a more compact statement summarizing concisely the repetitions and transformations that make up that activity.

So, within weeks, my students have discovered a model for the products of their writing that is at once correct and dynamic, rigorously clear yet lively and purposeful. It is also a real model, not an abstraction—one that they can build for themselves and one that they are in fact practicing regularly.

As the programming assignments become more complicated, my colleague from computer science begins to introduce our students to the process of structured programming. To give you an idea how this process works as a metaphor for composition, I will describe four stages of the programming process and explain how I use them in my writing class as models for analogous stages in the composition process.

The metaphors of structured programming, as I have said, are metaphors of design and construction. My students learn to begin the process of designing a program by creating something like a blueprint. In architecture, a blueprint represents the concept for a proposed construction; it is a miniature but complete and well-proportioned design of the whole. The blueprint for a structured program is called an algorithm. The term *algorithm* comes from mathematics; in computer science an algorithm is the idea or pattern of the steps by which a program processes its data and generates its output. An algorithm that describes a solution to the triangle problem, for instance, is:

[7] Linda Flower, *Problem-Solving Strategies for Composition* (New York: Harcourt Brace Jovanovich, 1981).

Set "space" to eleven units and "star" to minus one unit;
*
Reduce space by one and increase star by two;
Write a line of space-star-space;
*
Repeat between *'s nine times.

Here the data that were input were the two printing commands, space and star, and the output was the triangle pattern. Anyone who knits will realize that knitting instructions are often systematic algorithms of change and repetition similar to this one. The language of the algorithm consists of English nouns and verbs, not Pascal. Here we are concerned about thinking, not coding.

The concept of the algorithm has become useful for me as a teacher of composition in several ways. First, I teach students to think in terms of algorithms rather than thesis statements. Thesis statements are static summary sentences that students generally elaborate into those repetitive three-part essays. Algorithms, on the other hand, are patterns of argument and plans of action. I practice generating algorithms with my students in class by making an algorithm the goal of each discussion hour. At first this goal is indirect: I fill the blackboard with the key terms the students generate and (without telling) *show* them, by the way I map, connect, and separate their words, that they are gradually discovering the language and the pattern of a collaborative argument from which in fact an essay might emerge. Eventually the sense of finding direction out from the flow of conversation becomes a conscious student activity, and the students tell me where to place their ideas in the context of those of others. (Needless to say, this technique is pedagogically risky; it works better some days than others, and there is no guarantee that any particular class session will be successful.)

A second strength of the algorithm is that in computer science it represents one solution to a programming problem, but not necessarily the only solution. There are numerous programming algorithms for sorting a list into alphabetical order, for instance. Those algorithms are not all equally "good," which generally means not equally efficient at performing the sorting task. More complex algorithms, which result from imaginative analysis of the sorting problem, tend to produce better programs. Thus a "bubble-sort," which resembles a mechanical rearrangement of words by a series of one-at-a-time comparisons, is easier to conceive as an algorithm but markedly inferior to a sorting algorithm which builds a branching "tree" of the words as they are sorted and requires far fewer comparisons before it finds the proper place for each word. In the programming class, students advance through several sorting algorithms, from simple to complex, and are taught to judge the differences in quality among them.

So also are there numerous composing algorithms for analyzing a sonnet by Shakespeare or for designing a pamphlet on arms control. In class or at home, students can generate multiple algorithms to solve one composing problem. They generally begin by creating a descriptive algorithm that reiterates or imitates the structure of the subject: "In line one of Sonnet 73 Shakespeare says . . . , then in line two he says. . . ." When asked to reformulate, they create an analytic algorithm that imitates the process by which they have come to some understanding of the subject. "In Sonnet 73 Shakespeare describes three scenes about time:

[description of three quatrains]; he concludes that, because time is destructive, we should make the most of what we have; he uses effective images to prove his point: [list of examples]." Pressed harder, students can finally produce an integrated or synthetic algorithm that no longer imitates either the object or the process but which represents the structure of their own understanding. "Shakespeare describes powerfully the negativity of time: images of season, day, and hearthfire show that time is running down; images of ruined choirs, night, and ashes show that time yields death. But ironically, this negativity has the positive effect of strengthening love." This pedagogy of generating multiple algorithms, which is simultaneously being undertaken in their programming class, shows students how to reformulate and solve their problems at increasing levels of complexity and sophistication.

Having formulated a good algorithm, the programmer's next step is to develop that algorithm into a hierarchically organized scheme. This stage of the process is called top-down design. It entails complete articulation of the strategy sketched by the algorithm. Programmers begin "at the top"—that is, with establishing the logical relationships that will govern the overall structure of the program. Only then do they consider how to design the details of particular steps or procedures. This crucial concept of organizing first and foremost at the level of argument is alien to my students. For them organizing has meant arranging notecards full of quotations— the very pieces they will use to "fill up" the pages they must write. The technique of accumulating small pieces in the hope that they will all add up to something is derided by practitioners of structured programming with the term "bottom-up" programming. I am aiming to replace a bottom-up metaphor for composition with a top-down metaphor, and I do this with a tool that enables students to see the product of effective top-down design.

To help students organize an argument, teachers of writing traditionally introduce them to some schematic pattern or format for visualizing the relationship among the points that need to be made. This format is usually one version or another of the conventional outline. Programmers have at their disposal what I consider a more powerful and effective tool than the outline for organizing their writing, one that enables them easily to practice good principles of top-down design. This tool is called the Warnier–Orr diagram (Figure 4.1). First adapted for composition classes by my colleagues at the University of Montana, the Warnier–Orr diagram is a grid that presents an explicitly two-dimensional pattern for displaying the outline of a piece of writing, be it program or composition. Like the outline, the Warnier–Orr diagram format assumes that organization means a hierarchical arrangement of ideas according to patterns of parallelism and subordination. Unlike the conventional outline, the Warnier–Orr format makes it very difficult for a student to pretend that a linear or serial organization is really a hierarchical plan, because it is so easily "read" both vertically and horizontally. The vertical axis of the Warnier–Orr diagram reveals the argument that encompasses and organizes the composition at each stage. The horizontal axis describes how each portion of the argument is developed in detail. There is an excellent article on the use of these diagrams for composition by Harrington and Walton in the December 1984 issue of *The Journal for Technical Writing and Communication*.[8]

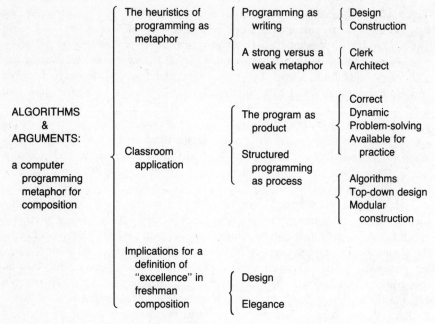

Figure 4.1.   A Sample Warnier-Orr Diagram

Thus far the programming metaphor for the writing process has suggested methods for planning and for design. When programmers finally begin to draft or code their programs—that is, when they begin to write Pascal words and sentences—they are not likely to proceed linearly from introduction to conclusion, from the first BEGIN to the last END. Instead they are likely to follow their top-down designs, first coding the pieces of the argument that shape the largest movements and then moving toward the articulation, the coding, of specific details. They pursue what they call a modular style of drafting programs; their programs are series of self-contained procedures or parts that are linked carefully by connectors called parameters to the central structure of the program. I have encouraged students to experiment with a similar modular pattern of drafting their compositions, especially the longer ones.

With so much recent emphasis on the power of the computer to assist students in the stages of invention and revision, we have given less thought to the critical stage of drafting and to the way different styles of drafting might affect both the substance and the effectiveness of the writing itself. Drafting a composition in small units and not necessarily in linear sequence, for instance, offers some interesting advantages. By beginning with a difficult central point in the argument, a student may clarify the point for herself; by discovering the rhetoric and diction that articulate a crucial turn, she may find the terms that best govern the expression of the whole piece. By focusing sharply on each individual unit of the argument, the student is likely to develop it more completely. Perceiving the need to place each

[8] Henry R. Harrington and Richard E. Walton, "The Warnier–Orr Diagram for Designing Essays," *The Journal of Technical Writing and Communication* 14 (3) (1984): 193–201.

part firmly in the structure of the whole, she also comes to recognize the power of effective transitions.

This modular style of writing is also valuable in getting both programmers and composers over the hurdle of how to begin. The programmer of Pascal has a rigid format for her opening: She must define fully at the start every term she is going to use. But how does she know before she writes what words she will need? The composition student has apparent freedom to design any opening, but if the opening is to *work right*, it should point the reader in the right direction and set up the vocabulary that the essay will utilize. When both programmer and composer begin to write away from the opening, they do indeed use, and therefore find, their proper language. The opening may well be the last module or paragraph to be completed, the language and direction for it having been gathered throughout the whole drafting process.

Finally, my students learn that the programmer has, in effect, three readers, three audiences. The first is the machine, which accepts the logic and sequence of the program (when it is correct) with full and unquestioning agreement. The second is the human reader, who uses the program for some purpose, be it business or pleasure. This reader judges whether the program is acceptable by the quality of its performance and the accuracy of its output. Finally, there are a few human readers who might actually read the Pascal code, which neither of the first two audiences do. These last readers are colleagues—other programmers who might be more skeptical—reading in order to understand or modify the sequence of Pascal statements. To make the extremely terse language of the program easily accessible to this third human audience, Pascal and other high-level programming languages allow the programmer to insert comments in natural English. These comments are typically set to the right of the Pascal code, separated by special brackets so that they are not read by the computer at all. They serve to augment, to explicate, or to highlight lines or paragraphs of code. Thus programmers are encouraged to anticipate the needs of the human as well as the machine audience and are granted freedom from the rigor of the artificial language in order to meet those needs. In my composition class, by the end of the term, my students are clearly ready to think beyond the validity and organization of their arguments to a similar consideration of their audience. As an exercise, they submit a draft essay in which they separate into parallel columns their "code" (the briefest, clear, unadorned articulation of the argument) and their "comments" (all the verbal devices they might employ to make their argument accessible and convincing to their audience). This distinction makes sense to them as programmers, and it helps to remind them as composers that the effort to reach a chosen audience can be both conscious and controlled.

The four aspects of the programmer's methodology I have briefly described— the use of algorithms, top-down design, modular construction, and commenting— are strategies I have found conceptually intriguing as well as practical for my students. But if we model a writing process on the heuristics of programming, how have we modified our definition of excellence in writing? If the metaphor changes, does the product? When I began to investigate this problem, the programming metaphor only suggested to me a kind of writing whose chief virtues were terseness of style and practicality of purpose. But I have come to recognize a more important excellence that I would call elegance of design. I emphasize design because for me programming is, above all, an act of creating significant order. But with structured programming I can add to design a classical ideal of elegance. For mathematicians, elegance connotes beauty through compactness, symmetry, and precision. In good, structured programming, that sense of mathematical or logical beauty is wed to an ease and clarity of communication that renders explicit and unambiguous even the most complex and subtle turns of argument. These virtues of design and elegance in writing are not the only ones I value, but they seem to me the right ones for college freshmen to aim for in their prose.

Text-to-Voice Synthesis

What We Can Learn by Asking Writers to Proofread with Their Ears

ELAINE O. LEES

When we teach inexperienced writers to edit their work for errors (an activity I will refer to, at times, as both "proofreading" and "editing"),[1] we customarily represent that activity as a matter of checking "real" text against intended text, checking the text on the page against the text in the writer's mind. Although recent theories of reading stress readers' active role in producing what they see as "in" a text or "on" a page,[2] our customary representation of error hunting at first seems adequate: It feels correct to skillful proofreaders and helps novices imagine the task before them. But this representation glosses over the part that readers, even proofreaders, play in "creating" what they read; it suggests that locating parts of texts that need change involves seeing texts as they really are, rather than bringing to bear on them particular interpretive strategies. Such a representation obscures the fact that each reading of a text (including a reading that identifies the errors it contains) is someone's reading—a reading embodying a particular strategy and point of view—whether or not others share that strategy and point of view. Like other readers, any editor comes to know what's on the page by performing acts of interpretation.

This essay explores what happens when proofreading brings together two interpreters of texts, two sorts of readers—one a human writer sensitive to meaning but lacking skill in handling textual conventions, the other an electronic text-to-voice synthesizer enacting conventions that transform writing into sound but lacking a sense of its powers' significance. After contrasting the human reader with the text-to-voice synthesizer, I'll show how working with a synthesizer appeared to help one student writer locate writing errors that he did not perceive when he worked alone. Finally, results of several studies of the effects of text-to-voice assistance on the editing of inexperienced writers suggest applications and further research.

---

[1] "Proofreading," because this activity appears to involve careful comparison of intentions and results; "editing," because it falls within the larger category of examining details of the text with an eye toward changing them for the better.

[2] According to Stanley Fish, for example, reading requires that a reader enact an "interpretive strategy," a strategy "not for reading (in the conventional sense) but for writing texts, for constituting their properties and assigning their intentions" (171). Because reading involves "constituting" the properties of texts, "giving texts their shape" rather than discovering properties and shapes self-evidently present beforehand, we cannot, in Fish's view, regard reading as a matter of coming to see texts "as they are" but must rather regard it as the creating of (more or less useful) interpretations (Fish, 168).

THE HUMAN READER AND THE MACHINE

By the time we reach college, most of us can interpret any given text at least two ways. We have mastered a way (sometimes several) to establish the "gist" of the text, to decide what the words on the page say to us. And we have mastered (at least to some extent) a different sort of interpretive strategy, one that enables us to assess the "correctness" of the text, to proofread what we read and locate errors in it. For even the most careful readers among us, these interpretive strategies tend to interrupt and derail each other. In the midst of reading for the gist of a passage, we slip into proofreading and—momentarily distracted from the sense of what we're reading— notice a spelling mistake. Or in the midst of proofreading, we slip into meaning- reading and overlook an "obvious" grammatical error. It appears that, when we employ one of these strategies, we hold the other in rather precarious abeyance.

Elsewhere, I have termed this ability to shift between readings "hetero- textuality" (Lees, "Proofreading as Reading"), and I think it's a trait human readers share. The reading machine whose effects I've examined over the past two years embodies only one interpretive strategy, however, so it cannot slip from that frame into a different one. By presenting texts in an alternative mode, the auditory, it reduces the reading tasks of editing and, most important, empowers editors who can listen more skillfully than they read and write. Because it differs in these ways from an ordinary human proofreader, under some circumstances the text-to-voice syn- thesizer may prove useful to novice editors.[3]

A text-to-voice synthesizer reads texts aloud. The system I've used, a Kurzweil Reading Machine, was originally designed to read books and typed materials to the blind. The machine employs an on-board computer to decode text and generate audio signals. The Kurzweil machine arrives at its reading of a text by scanning a page until it encounters print. Then it identifies characters, groups them into words, determines (with the aid of a dictionary of linguistic rules) how the words are likely to be pronounced in English, and finally notes punctuation marks and adjusts inflection accordingly. Because the Kurzweil uses its rules to "sound out" what it sees, it pronounces misspelled words and nonwords along with conventionally spelled ones, it pronounces syntactically tangled sentences along with smooth ones, and it tailors its inflection to fit unconventional punctuation along with conven- tional punctuation. For a composition class, the machine's performance of a stu- dent's draft can then be recorded on cassette tapes and returned to the writer for use in editing.

Such a machine has its shortcomings as an editing tool. The Kurzweil must read finished, typed texts, for instance, so it cannot keep up with writers' revisions. In addition, the machine's performance highlights only those features of texts that are sounded. Speech synthesis, then, cannot help writers detect homonym substi- tutions, phonetic spellings, or most punctuation errors. And though its readers are more accurate than those of many other synthesizers, the Kurzweil machine also occasionally mispronounces a word. The machine can "misread" when it encoun- ters a word not adequately handled by the rules in its program. It can also "make

---

[3] For additional discussions of text-to-voice synthesis and editing, see Lees, "Proofreading with the Ears" and "Using Text-to-Speech Synthesis to Assist Poor Editors."

mistakes" in reading texts when their print style is in some way ambiguous. Finally, the Kurzweil Reading Machine costs more than most luxury automobiles, but this drawback may be offset by the machine's availability in public and university libraries.

Even with its shortcomings, however, the machine provides opportunities to explore whether hearing a computer's interpretation of a text makes a difference in an inexperienced editor's sense of what is on the page.

ONE NOVICE EDITOR'S USE OF TEXT-TO-VOICE SYNTHESIS

Tracing the editorial changes made in a passage by one student, whom I'll call Lawrence, will suggest how a novice proofreader can make use of text-to-voice synthesis to locate errors overlooked in his ordinary proofreading.[4] Lawrence, a freshman enrolled in a first-level composition course at the University of Pittsburgh, proofread one of his papers (about 3 pages, or 580 words) 6 times: 3 times working on his own and 3 times using tapes of synthesized readings of his text. When he worked with the tapes, Lawrence made considerably more revisions than when he worked without them: He made 9 changes when he proofread alone and 36 changes when he proofread with the help of machine readings. The alterations Lawrence made in one paragraph of his paper are representative of his work on the text as a whole. (See Appendix.) Here are the paragraph's first two sentences as Lawrence originally wrote them:

> During the adolescent senior year of high school he endure some kind of mental or physical pain. And this usuall turns out to be significate for him.

Let's consider first what happened when Lawrence, following the advice of his basic writing teacher, read this part of his paper aloud as he proofread it. The following transcript shows Lawrence orally constructing a reading of the text that maintains its sense but may not represent its word-and-letter features in a way that helps him spot unconventional forms. Lawrence here appears to be reading to confirm his meanings; his reading miscues usually preserve the text's semantics or vocally correct what his readers would regard as errors in the writing.[5]

> During the adolescent years, senior year of high school, he endure(s)[6] some kind of physical or mental pain. And this usually turned out to be significant for him.

Before working with the text-to-voice tapes, Lawrence was asked to edit the paper three times on his own, making whatever changes he felt were needed. On the first round, Lawrence read the text silently; on the second and third rounds, he

---

[4] I have written elsewhere of large changes some writers made in their texts with the aid of text-to-speech synthesis. See Lees, "Using Text-to-Speech Synthesis to Assist Poor Editors," 200–203.

[5] For discussions of reading miscues, see *Miscue Analysis: Applications to Reading Instruction*, ed. Goodman; and *Findings of Research in Miscue Analysis: Classroom Implications*, ed. Allen and Watson.

[6] To write a transcript is also, of course, to interpret. I have tried to record faithfully my sense of what Lawrence said, yet ambiguities persist. Here, for instance, the initial sound of *some* prevents our knowing whether Lawrence said *endures* or *endure*. And later in the paragraph, in less tricky contexts, I'm not certain Lawrence sounded every inflection I think I hear on tape.

read the text aloud. At that point, after three rounds of editing the passage without the assistance of the text-to-voice synthesizer, Lawrence had produced a revised text. Numbers indicate the editing round on which a given change was made. As the absence of (2)'s indicates, Lawrence made no alterations of the text during his second round of proofreading (the round transcribed above). Before the third round of work, he received explicit instructions to read slowly and carefully.

> During the adolescents (3) senior year of high school he endure some kind of mental or physical pains (3). And this usuall turns out to be significate for him.

In some ways this revision is remarkable. In it Lawrence rather subtly manipulates convention—changing the noun *pain* to the plural and elsewhere choosing to add an article and to place a comma after an introductory phrase—while he preserves stretches of prose ("Haven to watch the game on the sidline was an sigmificat experiences for me") whose unconventionality startles most of his readers (see Appendix). The transcript of Lawrence's oral reading of his text suggests how he might have experienced what he'd written—though it's risky, I think, to assume identity between his oral performance and his experience of the text. Yet after three rounds of independent editing, it seems clear that Lawrence had not yet experienced some parts of his text as startling, though his readers would stumble over them. He hadn't yet seen his text in a way that would enable him to notice and repair what others would regard as basic errors.

When he had finished editing alone, Lawrence was introduced to the text-to-voice synthesizer. He was given tapes of the Kurzweil machine's reading of his paper and was instructed to make whatever changes he felt were needed during three more rounds of editing: on the first round, the machine read the paper at conversational speed; on the second, at a slowed-down rate of approximately one hundred words per minute; and on the third, at the rate of one word per second. Lawrence was working on a passage he had proofread three times; he had already made five changes. Nonetheless, on the first round with tapes he made three additional changes; on the second round, five more changes; and on the third, three more—for a total of eleven new changes, about two-thirds of which could be considered corrections of errors. In this final version, Lawrence attends to what he now seems to see as problems in the endings of words: More than two-thirds of his revisions involve final syllables. In addition, most of these changes are morphemic, suggesting that Lawrence controls some patterns of written-word structure more fully than we might otherwise have thought. Here are Lawrence's sentences as he edited them with text-to-voice assistance:

> During the adolescents senior year of high school he endures (2) some kind of mental or physical pains. And this usually (2) turns out to be significate for him.

Lawrence's performance with the assistance of voice tapes suggests that he knows more about conventions of written language than his unassisted editing reflects. When he works alone, Lawrence appears less inclined to question word forms in his text, but the forms he had found acceptable in his own reading of the passage no longer seemed acceptable when the machine read it. Hence it seems worthwhile to examine how voice assistance affects other novice editors' readings of their work. Would voice assistance help them re-see their writing?

COMPARATIVE STUDIES OF EDITING WITH TEXT-TO-VOICE ASSISTANCE

At the 1984 Minnesota Conference on Computers and Writing, I reported on a group of preliminary studies I had made with writers like Lawrence (a total of six writers, editing nine of their own papers—first without the help of synthesized readings and then with such help). At that time, I reported that the writers I studied made roughly twice as many changes and corrections when they edited with the help of synthesized speech than when they edited without it (see Lees, "Using Text-to-Speech Synthesis"). In the following year I extended this preliminary work in two further studies: first, to see whether text-to-voice assistance helped writers edit texts composed by others; second, to examine whether effects obtained with the synthesizer arose from writers' repeatedly editing the same text or from the use of the synthesizer itself.

In the first study, two groups of twelve students in a basic reading and writing course (a first-level course for inexperienced writers) proofread a standard paragraph containing numerous errors. Students in Group I were given tape players and cassettes containing a machine reading of the passage; students in Group II worked without machine help. Because preliminary studies had suggested that writers found the hundred-word-per-minute reading speed more helpful than slower or faster rates, that speed was used. The results of the study are summarized in Table 5.1. The mean scores for changes (alterations of any sort in the text) and corrections (alterations of an unconventional form to a conventional one) by the group using tapes are slightly higher than those for the group working alone. Because of wide variance among individual performances in this study, however, the differences in mean scores are not statistically significant. It may be that, when students edit texts written by someone else, listening to a taped text-to-voice performance doesn't make much difference.

A second question not addressed in the preliminary case studies was whether the increase in changes and corrections that occurred when writers worked with synthesized readings arose from the writers' growing familiarity with the texts they edited. In the preliminary studies, all writers worked with synthesized speech after they had first edited without machine help. Perhaps *any* repeated editing of a text would produce effects similar to those obtained when writers worked with the synthesizer.

Table 5.1. Effects of Text-to-Voice Assistance
on Writers' Editing of a Standard Passage

Group I (using text-to-voice tapes) $n = 12$
   Mean changes $= 30.42$ SD $= 8.06$
   Mean corrections $= 18.25$ SD $= 4.17$

Group II (without text-to-voice tapes) $n = 12$
   Mean changes $= 27.25$ SD $= 5.00$
   Mean corrections $= 16.58$ SD $= 4.87$

To explore this question, I had two groups of six students edit their own papers in two modes. Group A edited papers first with text-to-voice help and then without it; Group B edited papers under those conditions in the reverse order. Again, tapes were recorded at the synthesizer's hundred-word-per-minute reading speed. The results of this study are summarized in Table 5.2. To adjust for varying lengths of student papers, results are expressed as changes and corrections per hundred words of text.

Here we see little difference in the performance of the two groups on the first round of editing. Both averaged about four changes per hundred words, and about one and a half corrections. On the second round, however, the group using synthesized speech averaged three times as many changes and corrections per hundred words as the group working alone, and these differences are statistically significant at the .02 level for changes and at the .05 level for corrections. (One reason why the level of confidence is lower for corrections is that half the writers in Group A made zero corrections during Round 2, when they worked without tapes, boosting the standard deviation.) In the second round of writers' editing their own papers, we see once again a considerable difference in performance between writers using synthesized speech and writers working alone. Here machine speech appeared to be more effective as a backup, a means of helping writers find parts of the text they wanted to change after they had edited it once. Working alone, however, did not seem to be so effective a backup to working with the machine. Under that condition, writers made fewer changes and corrections; some writers made none at all. (None of the writers in either group edited out all, or even most, of the errors in his or her paper on Round 1, so the low numbers for Group A and Round 2 aren't the result of fewer opportunities to revise.) On the second round, then, the synthesizer once again appeared to help writers sense problems in their work.

IMPLICATIONS FOR FURTHER WORK AND APPLICATIONS

These two studies, though suggestive, also invite further investigation. One unanswered question is whether voice-assisted editing differs from unassisted editing

Table 5.2. Effects of Repeated Editing of Own Text, With and Without Text-to-Voice Assistance

	ROUND 1 (WITH ASSISTANCE)	ROUND 2 (WITHOUT ASSISTANCE)
GROUP A (n = 6)	Mean changes = 4.29 SD = 3.41 Mean correc. = 1.43 SD = 0.57	Mean changes = 1.00 SD = 0.78 Mean correc. = 0.21 SD = 0.25
	ROUND 1 (WITHOUT ASSISTANCE)	ROUND 2 (WITH ASSISTANCE)
GROUP B (n = 6)	Mean changes = 4.11 SD = 1.48 Mean correc. = 1.83 SD = 0.77	Mean changes = 3.06 SD = 1.41 Mean correc. = 0.69 SD = 0.39

when both are used as backups for the same first-round process. To explore this issue, we might have two groups of writers edit without speech assistance during a first round, then provide voice tapes for one group on the second round. The studies raise a second question: What accounts for the delayed appearance of significant differences in performance with and without the synthesizer in the second study? The lack of significant difference between groups in Table 5.1 may be a first-round phenomenon, one that disappears when writers edit again in the opposite mode. A second follow-up study, then, might require writers to edit a standard text, following a two-stage pattern.

Judging from my informal observations, however, I suspect that synthesized readings *do* affect writers editing their own texts differently from writers editing others' work. If so, this phenomenon has two interesting implications.

First, it suggests that synthesized readings may help authors overcome egocentrism when they read their own texts by making the texts seem to belong for a while to another speaker, the machine. When that speaker "performs" the text in ways the author doesn't expect, writers more readily see problems in their own reading and may change their sense of what "really appears" on the page. Such an effect might also be obtained, of course, by having a human reader carefully perform the text for the author. But that approach has its own liabilities. Being capable of grasping the text's meaning, the human reader may unwittingly produce corrective miscues of the sort the author would. More probably, and much more seriously, the human reader may socially complicate the situation. The text's performance then occurs in the context of a relationship (student/teacher, peer/peer, or writer/witness), and this context imposes on the novice editor a new set of constraints that center on the reader's motives and objectivity. A reader who carefully speaks every error a text allows may appear hostile or satirical, out to get the text, desiring to expose or embarrass rather than help. By contrast, because it can neither judge nor remember, the machine preserves its social innocence; it can address egocentrism without jeopardizing ego.

A second consequence, if the machine affects writers editing their own work more than it affects writers editing others' work, is that the synthesizer thus differs from other aids used in teaching editing. Rules and grammar exercises, for instance, seem to affect writers performing tasks in workbooks but have questionable influence on the writers' own prose. Perhaps listening to machine readings gets at something seldom affected when we teach proofreading, something connected with writers' grasp of the ability of their own texts to speak for them but independently of them.

Because the machine is built to create a single reading of a given text, it cannot slip from one interpretive system to another. It mechanically embodies only one such system, a system for recasting writing into sound. It cannot overlook an error, then, by slipping from proofreading to "meaning reading"; it has no alternative readings that can disrupt the reading underway. The synthesizer cannot "read around" an aspect of text that falls within the purview of its rules.

These limitations on the synthesizer's ability to generate readings serve to enhance, not diminish, its usefulness to a human editor, and this fact makes it unique among computer-based editing tools. Other types of assistance—those that depend on a program's ability to locate and identify errors in a text—eventually run up against the program's limited grasp of natural language semantics. (A spelling checker, for instance, is likely not to catch whole-word substitutions.) But a text-to-voice synthesizer does not really catch errors at all; its user does. The synthesizer merely adds singlemindedness (and, in some cases, orthographic orthodoxy) to the process. As a result, the speech system's role as an aid to editors differs fundamentally from that of error detectors. The benefits of the speech system depend less on a program's understanding of natural language than on a user's linguistic competence.

It may be possible for teachers and tutors to use text-to-voice synthesis to clarify differences between accidents and errors, between a writer's linguistic performance and her or his linguistic competence. Working with synthesized readings may suggest where writers do not sense linguistic differences that others hear or may draw out kinds of changes and corrections we wouldn't otherwise know they could make. For instance, when Lawrence worked with taped readings of his paragraph, eight of his eleven revisions involved the endings of words. Moreover some revisions, including a hypercorrection, "leted" (for the past tense *let*), are not revisions that could be predicted from hearing Lawrence read the text aloud (see Appendix). Having seen these changes, however, we can better imagine the kind of tutorial help Lawrence might need—and the kind he certainly doesn't need—as he works on editing. Lawrence seems to know already that some inflections are silent to him but still must appear in writing for school; he seems less sure of when not to add such inflections. The "leted" he revised into his paper also suggests that Lawrence would not benefit from drills in what to do with his uninflected forms appearing elsewhere.

Perhaps the most interesting possibility, then, is that using text-to-voice synthesis in editing may help some writers become more powerful and independent, better able to make their writing do what they want it to do. Not only would such help protect writers like Lawrence from the well-intentioned but inappropriate "remediation" of workbooks and drills; it would also locate the impetus for revision where our beliefs about writing imply that it should be located: in authors' own ability to discover how they want to sound and what they want to say.

REFERENCES

Allen, P. David, and Dorothy J. Watson, eds. *Findings of Research in Miscue Analysis: Classroom Implications.* Urbana, Ill.: ERIC and NCTE, 1976.

Fish, Stanley. *Is There a Text in This Class? The Authority of Interpretive Communities.* Cambridge, Mass.: Harvard University Press, 1980.

Goodman, Kenneth S. *Miscue Analysis: Applications to Reading Instruction.* Urbana, Ill.: NCTE, 1976.

Lees, Elaine O. "Proofreading as Reading, Errors as Embarrassments." In *Sourcebook for Basic Writing Teachers,* edited by Theresa Enos. New York: Random House, forthcoming.

———. "Proofreading with the Ears: A Case Study of Text-to-Voice Performance of a Student's Writing." In *Collected Essays on the Written Word and the Word Processor,* edited by Thomas E. Martinez. Villanova, Penna.: Villanova University 1984, pp. 218–230. Reprint in *Collegiate Microcomputer* 3 (November 1985).

———. "Using Text-to-Speech Synthesis to Assist Poor Editors." In *Selected Papers from the Conference on Computers in Writing: New Directions in Teaching and Research, University of Minnesota*, edited by Lillian Bridwell and Donald Ross. Special issue of *Computers and Composition*, a joint publication of Colorado State University and Michigan Technological University (1984): 195–211.

APPENDIX

1. Student's original paragraph

During the adolescent senior year of high school he endure some kind of mental or physical pain. And this usuall turns out to be significate for him. I remember going into my senior year season I worked hard to prepare myself over the summer to take over the job as leader. After working all summer long our first preseason game came, it went pretty well. When the third season came about I got injured. I tried to go through a quick rehabilitation, but it would not work. Everytime I push myself it seemed to get worst. The first game of the season came alone and I had to view from the sideline. Haven to watch the game on the sidline was an sigmificat experiences for me. Well we lost that game and I felt that I let the team down.

2. Transcribed oral performance

During the adolescent years, senior year of high school, he endure(s) some kind of physical or mental pain. And this usually turned out to be significant for him. I remember going into my senior year . . season. I worked hard to prepare myself over the summer to take . . to take over the job of a leader. After working all summer long, our first pre-season game came. It was pretty well . . It went pretty well. When the . . When the third game came about, I got injured. I tried to go through a quick rehabilitation, but it would not work. Every time I pushed myself, it seemed to . . seemed to get worse. The first game of the season came along, and I had to view from the sideline. Having to watch the game on the sideline was a significant experience for me. Well, we lost that game, and I . . felt . . I let the team down.

3. Paragraph as edited without text-to-voice synthesis

Numbers indicate the editing round (1, 2, or 3) during which a given change was made.

During the adolescents (3) senior year of high school he endure some kind of mental or physical pains (3). And this usuall turns out to be significate for him. I remember going into my senior year season I worked hard to prepare myself over the summer to take over the job as a (3) leader. After working all summer long, (1) our first preseason game came, it went pretty well. When the third game (1) came about I got injured. I tried to go through a quick rehabilitation, but it would not work. Everytime I push myself it seemed to get worst. The first game of the season came alone and I had to view from the sideline. Haven to watch the game on the sidline was an sigmificat experiences for me. Well we lost that game and I felt that I let the team down.

4. Paragraph as edited with text-to-voice synthesis

Numbers indicate the editing round (1, 2, or 3) during which a given change was made.

During the adolescents senior year of high school he endures (2) some kind of mental or physical pains. And this usually (2) turns out to be significate for him. I remember going into my senior year season, (2) I worked hard to prepare myself over the summer to take over the job as a leader. After working all summer long, our first preseason game came, it went pretty well. When the third game came about I got injured. I tryed to go through a quick rehabilitation, but it would not work, (2) Everytime I push myself it seemed to get worst. The first game of the season came along (1) and I had to view from the sidelines (3). Having (1) to watch the game on the sidelines (2,3) was an sigmificat experience (3) for me. Well we lost that game and I felt that I leted (1) the team down.

Observations on a New Remedial Language Arts Course

JOHN C. THOMS

Some years ago, for a graduate seminar, I had to read a thirteenth-century metrical romance called *King Horn* (Sands, 15–54). The poem contained the barest narrative, the skimpiest character development, and the bluntest symbols imaginable. It was written primarily in trimeters, so most of its words were monosyllabic. I thought it so simple as to be almost not worth talking about.

During the seminar discussion, however, it was borne in upon me that the value of *King Horn* lay in its very simplicity. Most of the essential motifs of medieval romance literature were in the poem, without much in the way of sophistication to obscure them; seeing those motifs writ large in *King Horn* helped me later to see them more clearly in more complex works. That discussion became a touchstone for me. From it I learned that even apparently obvious things generally repay thoughtful examination.

This past year and a half, under a Title III grant at the New York Institute of Technology, I have been developing a five-credit, one-semester remedial language arts course—English 1007, Basic Writing and Reading—which includes a variety of regularly scheduled microcomputer activities. Oddly enough, the course keeps making me think of that medieval poem. In its initial conception, English 1007 seemed to me almost outrageously simple; as with *King Horn*, however, I have found its apparent simplicity to be the source of new insight into complex matters. This remedial course has helped me to see more clearly what I am aiming at in all my teaching.

The course is certainly not difficult to describe. Classes meet three hours a week in a conventional classroom and two hours in a computer lab. The teacher is present for the first lab hour; the second hour is for unsupervised work.

Computers are used in the course in several ways. Word processing helps students to brainstorm, organize, write, revise, and edit their papers. It also provides teachers with a tool for creating exercises in sentence-combining, paragraphing, sequence, conciseness, and so on. Other software programs supply drill-and-practice exercises covering various patterns of error. Still others aim at improving reading speed, comprehension, and vocabulary. A spelling checker highlights suspect words in word-processed texts, suggests alternative spellings, and permits students to correct errors quickly and to print them out in lists. A rhetorical invention program helps students to generate ideas for writing. And a touch-typing tutorial introduces and reinforces keyboard skills.[1] A major consideration in software selection has been

---

[1] At present, lab work is done on the Apple IIe. Course software includes the "AppleWorks" word processor, "Dasher," "Speed Reader II," "Word Attack," "Spell It," "The Sensible Speller," "Prewrite," and "Typing Tutor III." Fuller information on these programs is provided after my list of references.

adaptability: Most of the programs purchased for 1007 allow teachers to design and enter their own exercises for student use.

Because there is a computer station for every student, 1007's supervised lab sessions can become genuine writing workshops, with the teacher assisting students as they write. Back-to-back scheduling of supervised and unsupervised lab hours permits the teacher to explain new lab activities and unfamiliar software, to observe students as they begin work, and to correct the inevitable misunderstandings and missteps that accompany each new activity, before leaving students and lab assistants on their own. Such scheduling also gives students adequate blocks of time for meaningful work on the computer.

The computer lab is available beyond regular class hours as well, so the more serious students are able to use word processing to revise their writing over time. Open lab hours also allow slower learners to pace themselves in the use of computer materials and give absentees the chance to catch up on lab assignments.

Apart from its use of computers, English 1007 is grounded in ideas now widespread in our profession. It focuses on a familiar set of basic language skills. It emphasizes the writing process. It presents writing and reading as interconnected. And it uses textbooks to reinforce these approaches. Indeed, 1007 might be characterized as a rather obvious composite of these elements, with computer activities simply tacked on to the regular curriculum. In practice, however, the computer has established a new context for that curriculum, thereby effectively transforming it.

Students in 1007 encounter written language in textbooks and on the blackboard, in their own handwritten or printed essays, and in word processing manuals and software instruction sheets. They also encounter it on the computer monitor (with or without visible format commands); presented in full or partial screens of text, phrase by phrase across the screen, or in centered columns down the screen; accompanied or unaccompanied by graphic aids. They meet their teachers not only in conventional classrooms and faculty offices but also in the computer lab, where those teachers necessarily assume a less directive role, becoming resources to be called upon when needed, advisors rather than indisputable authorities. Finally, students speak about their experiences with written language and with computers, to one another and to their teachers, in class discussions, peer review sessions, and writing workshops in both the classroom and the computer lab. As a result of all this interaction, they seem to be taking more responsibility for their own learning, while making complex connections that are new to remedial language arts courses.

As writers, by connecting preliminary jottings on paper and fluid emanations of light on the computer screen with the dignity of print in a final draft, they are coming to understand what prewriting and revision are all about. They are learning to see their own writing as mutable. They are finding that writing can be a process in which one discovers not only ways of saying things but also the things one wants to say. And they are seeing their own writing as reading on the screen, gaining a measure of objectivity about it as it appears before them in neatly formed letters.

As readers of texts by others, they are learning to be flexible. They are becoming adept at constructing meaning from words in a variety of physical forms and semantic units. They are beginning to view both writing and reading as processes in which initial formulations are altered to fit emerging meanings, emerging contexts. And they are witnessing firsthand the utility of clear and direct written language, as they seek to extract immediately usable information from on-screen instructions, software manuals, and Xeroxed handouts.

Their teachers are also making complex new connections as they devise, present, witness, and then reflect on course activities. Harvard's president, Derek Bok, has speculated that the greatest benefit of the introduction of computer technology into education may be that it encourages more careful thought about how people learn (37). My experience with computers in 1007 supports that notion. I find myself thinking very carefully these days about what I am doing and why.

Computer experiences can be isolating and sterile, as anyone familiar with unimaginative drill-and-practice software knows. They by no means *must* be that way, however. A 1007 class in the computer lab is anything but isolating for either students or teachers.

Recently, after observing one of my supervised lab classes, my dean said it reminded him of a one-room schoolhouse. I had never thought of the comparison before, but I could see its aptness. In one corner of the lab, a student whose descriptive essay had lacked adequate supporting detail was getting new ideas onto the computer screen with the aid of a rhetorical invention program. Off to one side, two other students, both with serious problems in verb use and spelling, were working with a program called "Dasher," typing out sentences from a set of verb-form exercises that included spelling words they had missed on the previous week's quiz. At a center table, yet another student was using a program I had designed to explore the concept of levels of generalization—a concept he sorely needed to master for the argumentative essay due the next week. All around these four students, their classmates were working away with their word processors, either revising essays previously submitted or composing new ones. And in the middle of all this purposeful activity, I—a new species of marathon man—moved quickly from student to student, answering questions, offering suggestions, straightening out problems, or yelling for help from the lab assistants: keeping in touch, watching, listening, and learning how to teach the course.

Computers once made me feel profoundly uneasy. They seemed to epitomize impersonality, to point toward a grim future of technological efficiency and human isolation. Now I'm finding that the introduction of all those once-forbidding machines into my English class has led to a comfortable intimacy—the word is not too strong—between my students and me. And I'm pleased that my dean was reminded of the kind of classroom my Idaho grandmother taught in seventy years ago.

I thought again of the one-room schoolhouse when I was looking through *Involvement in Learning*, the 1984 Report to the National Institute of Education from the Study Group on the Conditions of Excellence in American Higher Education. One conclusion reached by that study group is that "learning technologies should be designed to increase, and not reduce, the amount of personal contact between students and faculty on intellectual issues" (29). Certainly, English 1007 has increased the personal contact between my students and me. But what are the "intellectual issues" involved in 1007? What am I really trying to teach in the course?

I know that the student population is already changing, and changing dramatically. More and more students are entering college with previous computer experience; many have computers at home. My wife teaches "Logo" to kindergarteners; the computer sophistication those kids will bring to their college studies can scarcely be imagined. Nevertheless, nearly all of the students coming into my 1007 classes are encountering word processing, if not computers themselves, for the first time.

I have a responsibility to these students. When I introduce them to computers and computer software, I am establishing a framework for further encounters with the new technology. I want to offer my students reliable guidelines to the future. I want to instill in them attitudes and habits of discipline that will see them through the technological changes that lie ahead.

I've been using computers to teach basic writing for a couple of years now, and how I introduce the course seems increasingly important to me. I've come to think of English 1007 as a kind of crustacean that casts its shell at the beginning of each semester, always emerging from its old shell looking a bit different from before. For a few short weeks thereafter, its body seems tender and pliable. I sense new possibilities and catch quick, exciting glimpses of the creature it might become. But then the shell starts to harden. One must make choices as a course unfolds, and each choice cuts off other choices, other ways of approaching the material.

This remark is obviously true of every course. But with English 1007 it seems particularly true. Once my students have a few weeks' experience in the lab, my power to shape their responses to computers is diminished. They come to their own terms with the machines. If I have done my job right, these students will continue to explore what can be done with computer technology. They will look for ways to adapt it to their own ends. If I've done my job badly and my students have decided that computers are just too confusing to be useful, then there's not much I can do. I've had—and lost—my opportunity to present computers to them for the first time.

My department chairman keeps reminding me that it's not my job to teach computer skills. And I know that, basically, he's right. Valuable class time should not be wasted by paying too much attention to the mechanics of word processing or other software. Computer use should neither obscure the essential curriculum nor deflect us from our proper responsibilities as English teachers.

But technology is already altering the writing process itself (Halpern and Liggett, 1–8). And increased time spent at video screens will clearly require new modes of reading. Traditional definitions of "literacy," perhaps inadequate already, will surely fall short in the years ahead.

We all have a lot of sorting out to do, and my students need me to have done some of that sorting out before I present computers to them. They need me to know, for example, what is most important for them to learn about word processing. They need me to help them find the most effective ways to enlist the computer in the service of good writing, by which I mean writing that attempts to go beyond mere fast-food efficiency (admirable though that may be) to offer instead some flashes of flavor, some subtlety of taste.

Although they come from a wide variety of backgrounds, students generally begin English 1007 with a long-standing dislike of writing and reading, and a belief that they can't do either competently. Often they remember some terrible teacher who convinced them they couldn't read or write well, made them feel bad about it, and in this way froze them at a certain level of failure. The students in 1007 are not stupid; sometimes they are very wise, with extraordinary life histories to draw on in their writing. They tend to be concrete, sequential learners for whom thinking is often the telling of stories—people who prefer visual language to verbal language. What do such students most need to learn about writing and reading?

Before anything else, these students need to learn hope and self-confidence. They need to learn that their terrible first-, or third-, or seventh-grade teacher was simply wrong about them. They can write, and write well. They can tell their own stories with a power that everyone else in the class will recognize. And they can move beyond simply telling stories to generalizing from them, and thence to developing coherent and substantiated argument. They can read the experiences and the ideas of others, and they can learn to comprehend a text's public meanings while also recognizing the value of their own private responses to it.

All communication begins in responsiveness. These students need consistent validation and reinforcement of their own capacity to respond. Their computers should be reliable and should be available when needed. The command structures of their word processors should not be too abstract or complicated. The software they are required to use should be well chosen, suited to their particular needs, and supportive of them—not punitive—when they make mistakes. Computer assignments should be presented to them thoughtfully. We should not overwhelm such students with too much at a time. We should applaud their successes at the keyboard. We should patiently guide them through frustrations until the computer has become an instrument of empowerment for them, a tool that extends their control over language. If all these conditions are satisfied, computers can be valuable allies in the teaching of hope and self-confidence.

But English 1007 cannot simply aim to make people feel good about themselves. At the end of the course, every student must take a minimum-competency exit exam that consists of writing an argumentative essay in response to a one-page reading passage. This exam is prepared and graded by the English department as a whole. Students who make too many errors on this exam must repeat the entire course. In the long run, too many errors in writing and reading will cause other teachers later on, and employers beyond those teachers, to give up on these students, to see them as limited, as hopeless. And then they'll be back where they began. So I try to teach them precision.

The computer is a useful ally here. Conventions of English grammar and syntax may once have been dismissed as of interest only to English teachers. The computer, however, will not work unless exactly the right sequence of characters is typed in. By drawing a parallel between the importance of syntax in the one instance and its importance in the other, I can easily reinforce the notion that habits of precision are worth striving for. And this springboard allows us to leap very naturally into some fairly high-flying talk about the nature and uses of all sorts of conventions. We talk about how certain kinds of achievement are possible only through an appreciation of limit and through mastery of rules. We talk about the origins of linguistic conventions—about fifth-century Germanic invaders of England and why Mercian became the precursor of the language most of us speak today. We talk about linguistic changes over time—about the politics of language in England after the Norman Conquest, why George Washington could get away with being a poor speller, and how *ain't* was a fashionable word among upper-class British gentlemen only sixty years ago. We talk about why some members of minority groups today grow up feeling bad about the language they and their neighbors speak and what linguists have to say about dialectical differences. We talk about reality and about obstacle courses.

I've introduced such connections into my basic language arts classes before, but now the context is different. Now my students approach this talk about conventions, rules, and precision from the vantage point of their concrete, sequential experiences in the computer lab, where they have begun to demonstrate their mastery over the machine. Now they view my talk from a different angle. They've witnessed firsthand the power of conventions and of attention to detail. They can now see a relationship between these ideas and their own needs as writers and readers.

There is one more large idea I try to communicate in 1007, one I now regard as the key idea of the course: the importance of translation. I teach a writing process and present a psycholinguistic approach to reading. Both models imply that there are many possible texts that may emerge when a human being sits down to write or read, and that to work with language is to translate it from one form to another until we find a form that will serve our immediate ends. In Foucault's words: "Knowledge consists in relating one form of language to another form of language" (40).[2]

How can I hope to capture in words the complex processes by which this essay emerged and assumed its present form? The most I can say is that, in preparing it, I had ceaselessly translated and retranslated a set of ideas until I felt reasonably satisfied with the results. But this is a truth of which my students can make good use. Typically, they enter my class convinced that writing is easy for writing teachers like me and that good writers get it all right on the first draft. They need to know the importance of trying out different possibilities. They need to feel free to keep translating, to keep playing with their ideas until they get them into forms that feel right, forms that will serve. They need to learn that such restless translation is all right, is good, is in fact what thinking and writing are all about.

The computer certainly helps my students learn the importance of translation. They translate their ideas from brain to paper to screen to print-out, or from brain to screen to print-out to scrawled-on print-out to screen to fresh print-out, and so on. They insert and delete and move text around on the screen. They endure my badgering for draft after draft—my attempts to elicit the true story, the telling detail, the right word—and they go back to their screens for re-vision, re-envisioning their own texts, learning for themselves what Heraclitus meant when he talked about rivers (Kirk and Raven, 196–197).[3] They encounter their writing

---

[2] I am indebted to Geoffrey Sirc for this quotation.

[3] "Upon those that step into the same rivers different and different waters flow . . . " (fragment 217, from Eusebius's *Praeparatio Evangelica* XV, 20). "Heraclitus somewhere says that all things are in process and

as reading—glimmering at them from the screen, or neatly printed on paper.

I tell my 1007 students that there are basically only four things to learn in college: concepts, vocabulary, facts, and the judgment to apply these appropriately to specific problems. Their job is twofold. First, they must learn a variety of strategies. To become better writers, they must learn strategies for prewriting, selecting and organizing, defining purpose and audience, composing, revising, and editing. To become better readers, they must learn strategies for pre-reading, finding main ideas, pinning down details of vocabulary and syntax, drawing inferences, and interpreting. To become better thinkers, they must learn strategies for relaxing, letting their unconscious and half-conscious processes work for them, playing with ideas before locking them into logical sequences. Second, through disciplined practice in writing, reading, and thinking for themselves, they must gain judgment about when to use which strategies.

I want to talk for a moment about two writers who might at first glance seem to be at the opposite end of the spectrum from the writers and readers I've been discussing. These are two of eight experienced writers who, a couple of years ago, were introduced to word processing and had their composing processes studied by a research team at the University of Minnesota (Bridwell *et al.*, 391–393). These two writers participated recently in a new study conducted by Geoffrey Sirc, in which they used word processing to perform a specified writing task in response to a published article and then watched videotaped replays of their own writing sessions, commenting aloud on what they saw.

Sirc tells how, during the video playbacks, these experienced writers "could not restrain themselves from pointing to the screen, putting their hands on it, gesturing from point to point on the screen, following the flow of their ideas" (6). He remarks on the way they "range[d] over their texts as if they were landscapes" (7). Most tellingly, I think, he quotes one of these writers, who stressed the importance of play in the writing process:

> I was just following whatever intuitive leads I stumbled upon, and not driving myself too hard towards any pre-set notion of what I should come up with. It was more playing with the material than really working it over. And for me, for prewriting, I do a lot of it that way, sort of casual, leisurely, just playing with the stuff I'm working on first. (9)

The other writer remembered "leaning back and stretching here [when he had decided to try to summarize the main point of the text he was responding to] as if to gear up for this important task," and Sirc comments on how "This image of Joel stretching back to focus, incorporating both mind and body into his writing task, lingered in my mind through my analysis of the experienced writers' accounts" (5–6).

The image has lingered in my mind as well. I want my students to learn what these two experienced writers know so well: to let themselves get deeply, even physically, involved as they write; to range over their texts as if those texts were landscapes; to play with language and ideas. In my 1007 classes, I think that

---

nothing stays still, and likening existing things to the stream of a river he says that you would not step twice into the same river" (fragment 218, from Plato's *Cratylus*, 402A).

computers are helping them to learn these things. Working with language on a computer screen, these students become so absorbed in their work, so focused on the task at hand, that they easily lose track of time. Moving the word processing cursor from place to place in a text file, they receive visual reinforcement of the notion of text as spatial expanse and implicit encouragement to explore that expanse. Inserting and deleting and repositioning text, they find it easier to play with possibilities. They seem to be enjoying themselves. We seem to be moving together in a good direction.

I realize that this is not a scholarly paper. Most of what I've done here is to tell stories, offer descriptions, and draw tentative conclusions from my experience. But English teachers today must deal with a constantly shifting educational landscape, with technology that changes daily, with new sets of expectations, new demands on us, and new kinds of courses. I think it's important that we tell one another stories about what's happening to us and to our students, as computers alter the ways in which we write and read and think about the world. I think it's important that our stories contain solid descriptive details and good metaphors, so that we can accurately communicate to one another the complexity of the experiences we are undergoing. If we want to understand what's going on in our new computer classrooms—and if we want others to begin to understand, and to join us in developing humane applications for the new technology—we must talk not only about keystrokes and test scores and word counts and syntactic embeddings, but also about how it feels to be teaching these new kinds of courses, and why we're so excited about doing it.

REFERENCES

Bok, Derek. "Looking into Education's High-Tech Future." *Harvard Magazine* May–June 1985: 28–38.

Bridwell, Lillian S., Paula Reed Nancarrow, and Donald Ross. "The Writing Process and the Writing Machine: Current Research on Word Processors Relevant to the Teaching of Composition." In *New Directions in Composition Research,* edited by Lillian S. Bridwell and Richard Beach. New York: Guilford Press, 1983, pp. 381–398.

Foucault, Michel. *The Order of Things.* New York: Vintage Books, 1970.

Halpern, Jeanne W., and Sarah Liggett. *Computers & Composing: How the New Technologies are Changing Writing.* Conference on College Composition and Communication. Studies in Writing & Rhetoric. Carbondale: Southern Illinois University Press, 1984.

Kirk, G. S., and J. E. Raven. *The Presocratic Philosophers: A Critical History with a Selection of Texts.* Cambridge: Cambridge University Press, 1967.

Sands, Donald B., ed. *Middle English Verse Romances.* New York: Holt, 1966.

Sirc, Geoffrey. "When Writers Read Their Texts." Paper presented to the Conference on College Composition and Communication (CCCC). Minneapolis, 20 March 1985.

United States National Institute of Education. Study Group on the Conditions of Excellence in American Higher Education. *Involvement in Learning.* Washington, D.C.: U.S. Department of Education, 1984.

Computer Software Used in 1007

"AppleWorks Integrated Software." Rupert Lissner and Apple Computer, Inc., 1983. Apple IIe, 128K recommended, ProDOS 1.1.1, disk.

"Dasher: An Answer Processor for Language Study." CONDUIT Language Series. James P. Pusack, 1983. Apple II series, 48K, DOS 3.3, disk.

"Prewrite." Mimi Schwartz, 1984. Apple II series, 48K, DOS 3.3, disk.

"The Sensible Speller for Apple ProDOS." Sensible Software, Inc., 1984. Apple Computer, Inc., 1983-84. ProDOS 1.0.2, disk.

"Speed Reader II." Davidson & Associates, Inc., 1983. Apple II series, 48K, DOS 3.3, disk.

"Spell It." Davidson & Associates, Inc., 1984. Apple II series, 48K, DOS 3.3, disk.

"Typing Tutor III." Kriya Systems, Inc., and Simon & Schuster, 1984. Apple II series, 48K, DOS 3.3, disk.

"Word Attack." Davidson & Associates, Inc., 1983. Apple II series, 48K, DOS 3.3, disk.

Engineers Becoming Writers
Computers and Creativity in Technical Writing Classes

VALARIE MELIOTES ARMS

Contemplating the results of a three-year grant that enabled me to teach engineering students technical writing with a computer lab, I am struck by how much I have learned about the thinking and composing processes of my students. Certainly the computer affected the students' response to the course and, from their accounts, improved their ability to formulate as well as to express ideas. As I read a new book by Donald H. Graves and Virginia Stuart, *Write from the Start: Tapping Your Child's Natural Ability* (E. P. Dutton, 1985), I am struck anew by how delicate and how easily damaged thinking processes are. Graves and Stuart found that children in kindergarten and first grade loved writing but that the school system's emphasis on teaching it as its components—grammar, spelling, paragraphing, and penmanship—quickly decreased their interest. I found that college students released from inhibitions about grammar, spelling, paragraphing, and penmanship regained a joy in creating a flow of words to express their ideas. Little did I realize how much the computer would do to foster creativity when I proposed to teach technical writing with a computer lab.

Creativity can be fostered, and the right environment and the right tools are essential. I believe that computers offer the right tools and that teachers are necessary to foster the right environment. Although creativity is difficult to define, the creative person has several well-recognized characteristics: receptivity to ideas, fertility of ideas, originality (unexpected responses), and flexibility (acceptance of the unexpected). Teachers are instrumental in fostering these personal characteristics, yet many despair of "teaching" creativity. Instead they teach cognitive skills such as making comparisons, drawing inferences, supporting arguments. This limited view of cognitive skills fails to recognize the whole psyche, the right and left hemispheres of the brain. One psychiatrist has noted that it omits the role of visual thinking, which is essential to creativity: "the phenomenon of imagery can no longer be ignored. . . . It plays a crucial role in the process of creativity."[1] The synthesis of images and words leads to creativity, and the computer offers us a tool that has the inherent ability to effect that synthesis. The problem is that teachers have to recognize that fostering creativity, not just cognitive skills, is within their purview. When I began teaching technical writing with computers, I did not expect to influence creativity.

[1] Silvano Arieti, *Creativity: The Magic Synthesis* (New York: Basic Books, 1976), p. 46.

What I had expected from the use of the computer in a course required of all engineering students was an increase in revision, an improvement in simple mechanics such as spelling, and a better attitude toward the course because it made the writing process efficient. What surprised me was the impact of the computer on the thinking process of a group of students who visualize concepts that English teachers tend to verbalize. Because of those surprises, I am now acutely aware of the problems that arise in using computers in a writing class. Moreover, I foresee a change in the role of the teacher and the use of writing in the curriculum.

My projections, as well as my awareness, are rooted in a large body of data from the project, which I began with the assistance of Drexel University and the Fund for the Improvement of Post-Secondary Education. In 1981, when I thought of using the computer in a writing class, I knew intuitively that the students at Drexel University would be motivated to write by the computers. Obviously, Drexel students had lived in a computer environment even before the requirement that each new student purchase a Macintosh personal computer was imposed in 1983. The campus had numerous computer facilities, and the cooperative education the students experienced in industry exposed them to the latest in technology. In my technical writing class, I lectured two hours a week; for the third hour, the students and I met in the computer lab. During the lab, students worked with the prewriting software "Create" to focus attention on audience and purpose, wrote ungraded rough drafts that their classmates and I criticized with positive reinforcement, and revised with software such as an electronic dictionary and the global-revision guide "ReCreate." The lab's popularity warranted offering all the students enrolled in technical writing the option of using the computer. Although the students gravitated to the computer lab, not all of the faculty shared their fondness for technology. Some of the teachers chose to adopt my class structure; others simply gave students access to computers, who then followed the tutorial in the lab manual on their own time.

I collected written evaluations from approximately 300 students when they took the class and after they graduated. I also solicited written evaluations from the 15 lab consultants and the 10 teachers who used the word processing lab and from the 30 engineering teachers who read papers that students had written on the computer. In addition, I kept a notebook of my own observations of students I taught and faculty members I trained to use the lab. These data undergird my evaluation of the impact of writing with computers.

On the basis of the data I collected, I predict that computers will alter our approach to education. By allowing for holistic learning, they will replace the emphasis on imparting a body of knowledge with an emphasis on developing an atmosphere that encourages rather than stifles creativity. Many educators have noted that "As the greatest single social influence during the formative years, schools have been the instruments of our greatest denial, unconsciousness, conformity, and broken connections. . . . Schools break knowledge and experience into subjects, relentlessly turning wholes into parts, flowers into petals, history into events, without ever restoring continuity."[2] From my experience with computers in our tech-

---

[2] Marilyn Ferguson, *The Aquarian Conspiracy: Personal and Social Transformation in the 1980s* (Los Angeles: J. P. Tarcher, 1980), p. 282.

nical writing course, and despite some current problems with them, I am convinced that computers, used under the guidance of a perceptive teacher, can help students overcome the fragmentation of learning to integrate a variety of cognitive strategies. And by helping students with the onerous chores of copy editing, the computer frees the teacher to perceive and respond to individual student needs. My expectations for the students and teachers have been met by other teachers in this new approach to an old discipline. The surprises are raves and are attributable in part to the fact that we had time to overcome current problems. Because of the synthesis of expectations, surprises, and problems, I project an atmosphere of creativity in the technical writing classroom: a new excitement for engineering students as they become writers and a new role for their teachers—in writing and engineering.

STUDENTS: EXPECTATIONS

As I had expected, the computer affected students' attitudes toward writing. The electronic wizardry is intriguing and its ease of use makes the task of writing less onerous. John R. expresses a typical student attitude toward writing at the beginning of a term: "I do not particularly enjoy writing. This is due to the fact that I almost always fall short of my expectations. Falling short of my expectations is caused possibly by high expectations (Pip, Sir) and more certainly by my lack of proper scheduling to incorporate time for two or three rewrites." Especially in technical writing, students often have important information to convey and want to communicate it clearly. By making the strategies of clear communication easy to apply, the computer helps students feel more confident of their writing ability. Because the computer has electronic aids immediately available, it becomes a partner. Many find that writing is no longer a lonely task; the computer is their companion. My student Paul, a confident writer only when he had a computer, reveals the role of the computer as helpmate: "The computer will align text." Note that he says "the computer" when, in fact, *he* must make the decision to align text. The writer must command the computer to do anything, but Paul and many others credit their computers with making an almost independent contribution.

Actually the computer is supplying help that might be available in other ways, but its immediacy is critical to the cognitive development of a writer. For example, before and after the introduction of the computer, my methodology in teaching writing classes has emphasized the composing process. With the computer, students have a reminder at their fingertips of what to consider as they prewrite (in the software package "Create") and as they revise (in "ReCreate"). Even faculty members who used the lab for their own writing commented on how they had used the software "because it was there," making use of the software's specific set of questions even though they already knew the benefits of prewriting and revising. Initially, students in the class have to follow my methodology for the composing process because every piece of writing must be checked off in the lab in a rough draft— either in hard copy or on the terminal. Still, they freely make comments like Joe's: "In the past I would spend little or no time revising my writings. With the aid of [the computer], I no longer find revising a document to be a chore." Graduates, interviewed two to three years after being in the class, continue to profess that they revise frequently but painlessly if they have computers on the job. I do not doubt their sincerity because, in my role as consultant to the senior engineering design projects, I have read hundreds of rough drafts by students who seize the opportunity to get a computer account and expert help not for a writing class, but for an engineering class.

Students' evaluations clearly support my initial expectation that, for several reasons, the computer would improve the students' attitude toward writing. This improved attitude is reflected in an improvement in receptivity and flexibility, which are important characteristics of the creative personality. The computer affects both receptivity and flexibility because it can show writers where a problem may exist, can make a change efficiently, and does not penalize the student for experimenting. Indeed, the very vocabulary that students use to describe their relationship with the computer connotes a sense of playfulness that contributes to the creative spirit of experimentation: "When I play with the computer," an oft-repeated phrase, says it plainly. For many of our students, it is the first time they have "played" with words or the juxtaposition of ideas. Varying a word or a paragraph is easy electronically, and the workshop ambience of the course elicits such playfulness. Because many students do not read very much, they are unaware of the richness of language and its nuances. For some of them, the availability of a thesaurus or a dictionary that can expand their vocabulary without interrupting the flow of ideas increases their ability to articulate those ideas.

An objective study of my students by an outside consultant, Professor Mimi Schwartz, details the change in attitude and composing strategies. Her "Research Report: Effects of Computers on Student Writers" submitted to the Fund for the Improvement of Post-Secondary Education as an appendix to my final report (Grant #0233, 1982–1984) compares the invention and revision strategies of students in the first computer lab class with those in a traditional class. Professor Schwartz summarizes her analysis of student questionnaires, interviews, and classroom observations thus:

> The findings suggest that computers make revision easier for several reasons: 1) the ability to rewrite without recopying; 2) the ability to reread clean texts free from crossouts; 3) the availability of CAI features such as the spell and the thesaurus programs; and 4) the greater ease in formating. Fluency and ease in invention are also increased by computer writing. Contributing factors include: 1) easier revision, which reduces anxiety in starting; 2) easier rereading of drafts, which facilitates new decision making; and 3) more speed and flexibility in inputting text, which stimulate play and fluency.

In looking at the evaluations students wrote after completing the course, I find the word *confidence* used frequently to describe the effect of the computer on their writing. Said Tammy, "Overall, I am more confident and more comfortable with myself as a technical writer and feel like I've made great progress in overcoming 'writer's block.' " That feeling of confidence inspired many to do more writing than they ever had. Their writing also included activities outside the classroom, such as writing poetry and science fiction stories for the literary magazine as well as a regular column in the weekly school paper. For students who generally lack the confidence even to consider submitting work for publication, this activity is noteworthy. It identifies the emerging creative personality, receptive to new ideas, flexible enough to replace old ideas, stimulated to find original responses based on knowledge.

STUDENTS: SURPRISES

Although I had expected changed attitudes about composing, I had not expected that the printed text, either on the screen or on paper, would have other psychological effects on the writer. With computer-generated text, handwriting chores no longer block creativity. I am surprised to find how many students hate the sight of their own handwriting. Time and again, they write as did Jim S., whose handwriting is "awful": "You can get sloppy and fake it with handwriting. But the computer makes a visual impact—at least you can see that the word is wrong." Students enjoy the "professional" look of the text, and they respond to it with professionalism—that is, they pay attention to the details of spelling and grammar. Because some researchers have found a tendency in students to equate such cosmetic corrections with the quality of the content, I cautioned students not to make that mistake, and they had a reminder in "ReCreate" to direct their attention to content for global revision. At least according to Paula, engineers are "perfectionists" who do not like to see, let alone work with, a messy page, even one they have written. The legible text makes it possible for them to think more clearly about what they have written. Their illegible handwriting had obscured their ideas in unreadable text; the computer presents their text clearly so that they can "see again" to revise.

Sherry Turkle examines a common willingness to accord the computer a personality, to see it as Paul did—a companion and helpmate that is somehow smarter than the user. The child she calls Tanya, a fifth-grader who could not write, exhibits the same inspiration my students claim once she acquires confidence in the computer's ability to help her write. Tanya had "very clear ideas about what is beautiful and what is ugly. She saw her handwriting as ugly and unacceptable. It made writing unacceptable. The computer offered her a product that looked 'so clean and neat' that it was unquestionably right, a feeling of rightness she had never known at school, where she was always painfully aware of her deficiencies, ashamed of them, and above all, afraid of being discovered."[3] The students I met felt the same fear of exposing themselves in their writing because their handwriting did not suit the sophistication of their ideas. Their fear of exposure clearly blocked their receptivity; the computer fostered their receptivity by producing an appropriate medium for their ideas.

A second surprise was as much social as psychological: Computers facilitate collaboration (see Arms, "Collaborative Writing with a Computer"). In industry, engineers typically work in teams and their written documents are reflections of the team effort. One person may do all the writing, which the other team members then critique. Or each member may write the section related to a particular area of expertise, and then someone edits all the sections for consistency in style and

[3] Sherry Turkle, *The Second Self: Computers and the Human Spirit* (New York: Simon and Schuster, 1984), p. 125.

diction. Although many college writing courses stress individual work, some engineering courses require that students submit reports written collaboratively. At Drexel the majority of engineering students receive a grade on a collaborative writing assignment, but they do not receive any instruction on how to write collaboratively. In the computer lab they discovered a way to synthesize individual sections for group reports and to edit with ease. With the computer holding the multiple versions of a group report, students could edit the report to achieve a consistent style for the entire document. More than 75 percent of the seniors voluntarily chose to use the lab for the required project reports in the year-long engineering design course. Voicing the sentiments of many seniors willing to wait in line if necessary to get into the lab, Greg said, "Any group member can come to the computer room and access relevant documentation . . . whenever his schedule allows. Also, he can easily review and edit any contributions made to reports by his fellow group members."

The engineering faculty members who assigned the collaborative reports were especially pleased to read reports written on the computer. They commented on improvements ranging from consistent typography to well-edited, coherent documents. It is significant that the College of Engineering has recognized the students' need for help with collaborative writing and now formally provides it by including me as a consultant for students and teachers in senior design. Thus the writing required for senior design projects gets the same kind of attention as the engineering.

The workshop atmosphere of the lab was also influential in developing the collaborations. In this respect the lab consultants were part of the team effort. I worked on fostering the workshop atmosphere by introducing the lab consultants as the people to ask if there were questions about the computer; I was "the writing consultant," and their classmates the engineering consultants (for help with acronyms, definitions, and analogies). In my training workshops, I stressed the need for positive reinforcement when lab consultants talked to the students and when students talked to one another. Criticism was to begin with the strong points and then to suggest ways of making the rest of a paper stronger. Another factor in improving collaboration was the clean text. Like many others, Ken commented that "it is much easier to suggest revisions when you know how easy it is to make those revisions." Finally, the computer facilitates collaborative writing because of its fast turnaround time; a revised text can be reconsidered and deadlines met to everyone's satisfaction.

A third surprise has great implications for the future of computers in writing: The computer encourages the synthesis of visual and verbal ideas. Further, it moves writing from the English class and distributes it across the curriculum. Students discover that writing is a cognitive strategy, *not* a subject matter, because of their interaction with the computer. With the computer as helpmate, students are able to explore ideas, to shape them, to refine them, and most significantly, to represent them with computer graphics. The strategy of using writing as a way of exploring is not specific to writing class assignments; it is a strategy that extends across disciplines and subject matters. The student working with the computer in each communication effort accrues knowledge, rather than segmenting it to a particular class. More important, the student can use all of her creative faculties with a computer. Because images are important in holistic learning, they can be encouraged, recorded, and integrated with the ideas expressed in words. Offering its graphics capability in conjunction with its word processing capability, the computer fosters "the magic synthesis": creativity.

By making holistic learning possible, the computer changes the students' thinking about writing. Although the computer can be compared to a typewriter because of the keyboard, it offers an additional sense of companionship, the indefatigable helper. The computer can also be compared to a television because of the screen, but it involves students for the first time in creating their own screens. Those same students have been passive viewers of screens all their lives, but they have never been able to interact with a television screen. The computer looks like a television screen, but it awaits their command. Its appeal is compelling, and it changes the view of writing as linear. As Gary found, the computer "allows one to place his thoughts at random then organize them—which is the normal thinking process." Said Bernie, "Now I think of writing as a mosaic—I move pieces around until they fit." Both writers are reflecting the impact of the computer on their thinking processes, not just on their composing processes. The computer goes beyond the gimmickry of word processing techniques to involve the senses in interaction, to involve both the right and the left hemisphere of the brain, which leads us to creativity.

As a logical outcome of writing for discovery, students profess to feel more creative when writing with a computer. Mike H. says the computer "lets you use your imagination as you create. . . . [It] is a valuable tool for learning and expressing thoughts." Those "thoughts" are literally highlighted on a computer's screen where they can be physically rearranged and examined. Rick S., a dyslexic student who taught me a great deal about the power of the computer in fostering the creative personality, said, "The computer gives me a window on my ideas." (See Arms, "A Dyslexic Can Compose on a Computer.")

The "window on ideas" concept is especially important because many people think visually. Looking over the writing samples of my students, I repeatedly found comments that echoed Rick's. For example, Conor, whose ideas came as pictures, said, "I found that most of the time I have good ideas, but some of these ideas get lost in the transition from the brain to the paper. . . . My grammer [sic] is very poor and my spelling is even worse." Bill said, "Often I have an idea that is not easily expressible in words but is perfectly clear in my mind." And Drew added, "When my visualization is complete, I physically organize my notes in the correct order. . . . When I have a clear picture of paper [in my head], I quickly write it in final or nearly final form." Don explained to me that he "thinks on the computer" by drawing his ideas in "Macpaint" and adding text. He draws boxes around text, drags it into charts, and finally moves into "Macwrite" when he has a clear picture of the paper in a diagram. These students—all engineers—could see their ideas but were hampered in transposing them into print. The power of the computer to let them use their visualizations is critical in their developing the conviction that they are now saying what they mean.

Our educational institutions are postulated on linear left-brain processes. "The left brain can organize new information into the existing scheme of things but *it cannot generate new ideas. The right brain sees context—and, therefore, meaning.*"[4] The students I have mentioned have been stifled by an educational system that has failed to take into account more than one way of knowing. Fortunately, the computer can integrate cognitive strategies. In particular, its graphics capability unleashes ideas and promotes flexibility.

Students recognize the improvement in their ability to communicate and make the composing process work for them in all their writing, not just in class assignments. In my encounters with former students who use the lab, I find them prewriting, writing, and revising assignments ranging from feasibility studies in thermodynamics to reports for materials lab. The same procedure for composing has many different applications. Just as the finite-element method can be used to analyze structures varying from skyscrapers to airplanes, writing is a tool for analyzing ideas or information on any topic. While this is obvious to English teachers, it is astonishing to engineering students.

Juniors and seniors asked to describe their writing experience frequently respond, "I haven't had to write anything since I took freshman comp." Apparently they do not count letters, memos, lab reports, or job application forms as writing. But the computer makes them count as writing, because the same formating software is on the computer ready to lay out any letter; the dictionary is available at the touch of one key; the prewriting and revising software can be followed to improve any piece of writing.

A well-designed study at the University of Washington supports the contention of the technical writing faculty and the engineering faculty that the papers written on the computer are better than those written conventionally. Anne Gere, who reported on the study at the UCLA Conference on Computers and Composition in May 1985, stated that the papers of students who wrote with WANDAH (software, now called "HBJ Writer," that is built on the composing process) scored statistically higher than a control group's papers, which were not written on the computer. (The scoring was based on primary traits, and the study included approximately 80 students.)

Students themselves are convinced of the qualitative difference. To illustrate my point, let me introduce two students who were obviously the products of good writing programs when they entered the class. Rick R. and Dave B., who wrote a collaborative report on a Macintosh personal computer, liked to write and revised extensively. They had both had a good background in English, yet they professed to write better with the computer because it made revision easier. When they submitted their report, they both excitedly insisted I page through the document to see how beautifully they had handled the format and graphics. It mattered greatly that the document looked professional; the text was equally professional. When I asked Dave whether the report would have been as good if he had written it conventionally, he answered, "No, the computer gives you the tools to expand your mind to the limits. You're not afraid to spend more time working on the computer." Clearly he and Rick had expanded their minds creatively in writing their report on the Macintosh.

For them, the graphics software of "Macpaint" was critical to the way they

---

[4] Ferguson, p. 297.

expressed their ideas. I interviewed them separately to probe the impact the computer had made on their thinking.

VMA: Were you thinking more visually?

DAVE: We knew we could do some tremendous visuals on the Mac. We knew what we could and would do with the Mac. Without it, we would have had much fewer visuals. We had in mind that certain parts of the paper we were going to include pictures.

VMA: Okay, so it's sort of built in by virtue of the fact you knew you were working on the Mac?

DAVE: Exactly. We probably would have had much fewer diagrams, maybe one or two, if we didn't have the tools at hand. We didn't feel that we were willing to lead up to the pictures. They were integral to the project, we referenced them, but we didn't build the whole discussion around them. We weren't just doing pictures for the sake of doing pictures because they were fun on the Mac. We made original versions and went back to edit the graphics four or five times.

Rick was even more awed than Dave by the power of the computer to help him communicate; thus he was inspired to go beyond anything he had done before.

RICK: A lot depended on the software, "Macwrite," which gave me the ability to make things very presentable as opposed to using the typewriter. It was an array of possibilities that we could use; we put headers and footers on each page. It was very presentable; it looked like a book, which was beyond anything I ever turned in before. Also, using "Macpaint" to put in the picture, it fit well with what we wanted to show. We were able to show exactly what we wanted to show. It was easy to do, with "Macwrite" and "Macpaint," hand in hand. We planned some of the writing around the pictures. We knew certain figures would be easier to present an idea than writing about that; it was sorta like an outline to a certain extent. You could draw people in to what you were trying to explain by using the figure.

Note that twice Rick says "presentable" to describe his paper and that he felt challenged to make the content match the appearance. Both Rick and Dave used the potential of the computer to expand and explore not only their ideas but also the best way of communicating those ideas. As good writers and knowledgeable computer users, they were more creative than they would have been without the computer. Although it is difficult to judge creativity, an experienced teacher can recognize that something unusual and exciting is happening when students are visibly delighted in their accomplishments.

In much the same way in which IBM's "Writing to Read" system allows children to write on the computer before they can handle the mechanics of spelling and penmanship, the computer in the technical writing class allows students to exercise the power of their imaginations, unfettered by what are properly known as editing problems. Because students writing on computers need not initially concern themselves with spelling, grammar, penmanship, or even coherent paragraphing, they are freed from censoring ideas to only those they can "correctly" verbalize. Instead they can begin with doodling if that is a stimulus for finding what they know—not just what they can spell. The combination of graphics in "Macpaint" and the word processing ease of "Macwrite" offers the possibility of holistic learning rather than compartmentalizing the pictures and the words; writers can integrate visualization with text to explain an idea.

The power students feel in being able to verbalize visual concept excites them; their former inability to find the words to express their ideas had limited the ideas they expressed. The experience is like that of a traveler to a foreign land: It is the difference between knowing only enough of the foreign language to ask for necessities and being able to conduct an intellectual discussion as in one's mother tongue. Especially for engineering students, who often begin with a conceptualization or physically design the product first, the computer offers opportunities heretofore unavailable to them to combine the visual dimension with the prose necessary to explain it.

As an artist friend, Bernard Brenner, has expressed it, the ability to control the tools expands the ability to create. Brenner, himself a sculptor and teacher, began playing with the graphics software on the computer his wife uses for accounting. His excitement grew with his mastery of the computer, and the complex art that he now creates and sells belies the notion that computer art is simplistic (see Figure 7.1). Recognizing the importance of his change in attitude as well as his sophistication as a computer artist, he kept a journal that he showed me during one of our many discussions about creativity:

> The creative process is the result of a synthesis of the external and internal worlds of the creator. An active and engaged involvement with "building" a statement visually is a superb method of encountering the creative process and becoming familiar and at ease with it. This is simply because the evolution of the process can be seen, felt, intuited, and at times recognized and conceptualized. Not only do we evolve in our ability to see, utilize, intuit, and understand the visual. At least equally important is the development of our skill in articulating, sharing, communicating, and using the experience of process thinking in an enhanced and vitalized way.

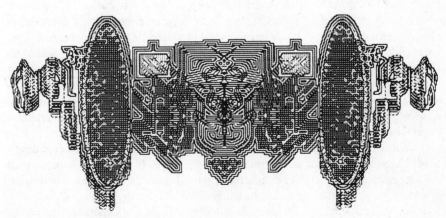

Figure 7.1.   A Sample of Computer Art.

TEACHERS: EXPECTATIONS

As I expected, teachers have responded to computers (1) by designing courseware that helps them achieve course objectives and (2) by evaluating software and hardware on the market and determining how best to use it. The surprise is that teachers are moving from the role of pedagogue to that of advisor, from teaching writing to fostering creativity. Many teachers are uncomfortable with their lack of computer expertise, especially when their students are more familiar with computers than they are. One teacher angrily refused to be part of my project, declaring, "I won't have anything to do with a machine that I can't understand!" But even if they know little about computers, teachers' knowledge of writing strategies and models enables them to advise students on their writing in ways that encourage creativity.

The computer can put the teacher in the role of a Socratic prodder rather than an error finder. With sophisticated software like "Writer's Workbench," the computer can identify possible errors in spelling and punctuation and even indicate possible overuse of passive voice and nominalizations. It can free teachers to encourage the exploration of ideas and the style best suited to communicate those ideas to a particular audience. One member of the technical writing staff commented that the computer eliminated the need for him to sell the course to his classes: "The computer gave the course a kind of electronic endorsement and stimulated several of the students immediately. . . . I am certain I received more carefully prepared papers than I would have without the program." He went on to add that he noticed a difference in his own writing when he used the computer: "I am more psyched for writing than I can ever remember." He was set to write "The Great American Floppy Disk" and, as an experienced writer, could only marvel at the excitement of writing on the computer that he shared with his students.

My own response to the introduction of the computer was to design courseware consistent with my objective of teaching writing as a process. Limited by the computer hardware, I found no existing software for a PRIME 850 minicomputer that guided a student through the composing process. With Hugh Burns's prototype, I designed a prewriting package, "Create." Burns has described his program in several places, but the most thorough description is his doctoral dissertation. My software is described in "Creating and ReCreating," *College Composition and Communication*, December 1983. Within a few months, I realized that students needed some help with global revision. Although the computer makes revision easy, many researchers have noted the tendency to focus only on the lines on the screen rather than on the complete document; hence I designed "ReCreate" to direct attention to overall organization and purpose. Finally, because no texts existed to introduce word processing as a writing technique, I compiled a manual that included a tutorial to introduce students to the computer.

Such work is primitive compared to courseware now available or being developed. Helen Schwartz has written an excellent textbook, *Interactive Writing*, which introduces computer activities concurrently with the writing strategies. The importance of the image has been acknowledged by Gabriele Rico in her "Course in Enhancing Creativity and Writing Confidence," which she expounds in *Writing the Natural Way: Using the Right Brain to Release Your Expressive Powers*. Researchers at UCLA and Carnegie Mellon have developed complete software packages that include word processing, prewriting, writing, revising, and diagnostic components specifically for college students who have access to IBM personal computers. Others, at the University of Minnesota and the University of California at Santa Barbara, are working on software that enables the teacher to alter a program's instructions to suit a particular class. Teachers are designing courseware to meet their needs from textbooks to software at every grade level. These people are not programmers or computer experts; they are teachers who are creatively applying their expertise to a new medium.

One colleague who wanted to create a software package for the Macintosh asked me what programming language she should learn. I assured her that she could design the software with no programming knowledge just as though she were writing a textbook with no knowledge of a printing press. I designed my courseware with the help of a computer science major; in effect, I did a storyboard and he did the "filming." The important question is not "What language should we use?" but "What can the computer do that we can't or shouldn't do in class?"

But teachers need not design courseware now that the market for educational software is expanding. Teachers need only use their well-honed skills to recognize a product that meets their needs. Reviewing software and actually working with it on a computer are similar to reviewing textbooks. Teachers can evaluate the courseware and choose whatever complements their class objectives. At Drexel, teachers can visit the campus Software Review Center, which, like a library, stocks various brands of computers and software for demonstration. Public libraries and universities across the country are now offering such facilities.

TEACHERS: SURPRISES

As teachers find themselves in the role of advisor evaluating the substance of student papers rather than the mechanics, they realize how much power the computer has to shape the students' writing. That power has to be countered to protect individuality. Because people attribute computers with infallibility, they often accept diagnostic advice from computer programs unquestioningly rather than recognizing that the "standard usage" on which such programs are based is itself questionable. Novels by writers such as William Faulkner, Thomas Wolfe, and James Joyce would not pass unscathed through a "Writer's Workbench" analysis. Whereas the best computer cannot recognize the artistry at variance with the norm, a good teacher could perceive the genius at work.

A more serious problem derives from the view of the computer as omniscient. A software program can indicate that a particular text varies from the accepted or recognized style. Students seldom question the need to conform to that style. Here the teacher must intervene to help students recognize their own uniqueness in relation to convention. But the task for the teacher is difficult because teachers, too, can become dependent on the computer and act as if it were omniscient. The myth of the omniscient and unfathomable machine may well grow with the use of expert systems and with advances in artificial intelligence. As humanists, teachers will be hard-pressed to define their own relationship to the computer in order to help students recognize the distinction between humanity and machinery, between creativity and convention.

Surprisingly, the role of the engineering faculty is also affected by students' responses to the computer as a writing aid. The software that guides invention and revision or flags possible grammatical errors is always available to the student, not confined to the writing class alone. As writing moves out of the writing class to become a tool for discovery in any class, it behooves the engineering faculty to incorporate it actively into their curriculum. At Drexel many have already done so, suggesting that students record notes about the labs on the disks with the data, make observations on field trips, freewrite to get going on seminar papers, and in general jot ideas, as they develop, beside the calculations. Responding to my questionnaire about the quality of the papers written on the computer, three engineering department heads and two deans were sure they saw an improvement because "papers are *obviously* being written two, three, and four times." Another engineer, who led a large seminar, included a personal testament: "When I bought my own computer three years ago I expected to use it about 85% of the time for analyzing data and 15% for word processing. I confess the ratio is completely reversed. I spend 85% of the time word processing and my publication rate has increased significantly."

The danger is that some teachers and administrators assume that the computer totally replaces the teacher. Research at the University of Southern California's Center for Instructional Research, Development and Training reveals that there is

> confusion about what an information technology can be expected to contribute to education. Generally, educators have failed to make a distinction between the teacher and the teaching. Any medium (including a human being) can serve as a teacher—a vehicle for delivering information. However, the delivery vehicle does not provide adequate teaching. It is the teaching that influences learning. Examples of teaching would be organizing lessons, using appropriate examples or analogies, sequencing facts, and giving the student corrective feedback.[5]

Though it is possible that good software can "teach," it is doubtful whether we could all agree on a perfect teaching program. Thus teachers must continue to be teachers— to encourage students and to refine solutions offered by new technology, just as they have for centuries with new tools like writing itself, which ended the oral tradition.

PROJECTIONS

Synthesizing the data I have presented—the expectations that have been met and the surprises for students and teachers—I am optimistic about the future of the computer in writing. In five to ten years, teachers and students will be adept at using computers, and computers will be readily available in libraries, schools, work places, and many homes. Sophisticated software will guide the whole writing process. There will be no need for a class to teach writing, but there will be a need for a teacher, perhaps as a consultant in a writing lab, to mediate the computer's advice and to help students

[5] Richard E. Clark, "Computers Can't Teach," *The Institute* (the newspaper of IEEE) 9 (1): 5.

explore ways to develop their creative personalities. However, with powerful software dictating conventional style, there is a danger that all writing will tend to a uniformity of style. I think that teachers bear the burden of discouraging such uniformity.

Evidently many teachers impose their left-brain orientation on students who are right-brain-oriented. Unfortunately, most of the courseware developed so far for computers reinforces left-brain activities and neglects the computer's potential impact on the right brain—and this despite the excellent graphics capabilities commonly available. Educators have already been forewarned of some of the dangers of this wonderful new technology. Gary Clark, in listing a dozen ways computers can be harmful, includes one way that is especially pertinent to our discussion: *"Computers are bad when they limit student–machine interaction to the left side of the brain; that is, to the more linear and logical activities"* [Italics his].[6] We need to devise ways of teaching that recognize the validity of what some educators are calling "transpersonal education." As Ferguson says,

> Unlike most educational reform in the past, [transpersonal education] is *imbedded in sound science*: systems theory, an understanding of the integration of mind and body, knowledge of the two major modes of consciousness and how they interact, the potential of altered and expanded states of consciousness. It emphasizes the continuum of knowledge, rather than "subjects" and the common ground of human experience. . . . It aids the learner's search for meaning, the need to discern forms and patterns.[7]

The computer provides a medium that is more akin to the thinking process of many people who see their ideas. Technical and scientific ideas are visually rooted in models, diagrams, flowcharts, blueprints, and equations that have a particular layout that designates the proof. Now, not only calculations but also visuals can enter into the initial communication of the idea. The computer short-circuits the linear approach to communication and allows a holistic approach.

A student gifted both as a writer and as a computer expert, Jim G., offers evidence of the computer's contribution to his creativity. He liked to compose science fiction stories, which he brought to me to critique. Realizing he was a creative personality with a command of the tools, I asked him to explain how the computer contributed to his creativity. His response follows.

> Word processing is not just a matter of deleting characters or printing documents. It is also a matter of the thought process. Pen and paper make the fingers tired. A typewriter needs new paper and can provide messy drafts when making numerous revisions. A word processor, though, allows you to think about what you are writing without interrupting the precious mental connections that a writer cherishes so highly and are broken so easily. . . . With no need to worry about when I have to hit the carriage return, or how much paper is left, or how sharp my pencil is, I can concentrate on writing. My thoughts are not interrupted by trivialities. The only interference left is the interface between fingers and keys. And maybe in a few years, even this will be solved.

With computers affecting students' receptivity and flexibility, teachers have the opportunity to *teach* in the true sense of the word—to encourage and stimulate their

---

[6] Gary Clark, *Computers and Young Minds*, (Chatsworth, Calif.: Datamost, 1984). Reprinted in *The Computing Teacher* 12 (May 1985): 8–9.

[7] Ferguson, p. 288.

students' ideas, to explore new concepts as well as new technologies. And with an awareness of the computer's power to incorporate visuals, teachers can include images in their list of cognitive strategies. The synthesis may seem magical, but teachers allied with computers can foster creativity.

REFERENCES

Arieti, Silvano. *Creativity: The Magic Synthesis.* New York: Basic Books, 1976.

Arms, Valarie M. "A Dyslexic Can Compose on a Computer," *Educational Technology* XXIV (January 1984): 39–41.

———. "Collaborative Writing with a Computer," *The Technical Writing Teacher* XI (Spring 1984): 181–185.

———. "Creating and ReCreating: Computer Composition Programs," *College Composition and Communication* PC-26 (December 1983): 175–177.

———. "Final Research Report: Innovative Teaching of Technical Writing with a Word Processing Lab." Submitted to the Fund for the Improvement of Post-Secondary Education (Grant #0233, 1982–1984).

Burns, Hugh. "Stimulating Invention in English Composition through Computer-Assisted Instruction," University of Texas at Austin, 1979, ED. 188245.

Clark, Gary. *Computers and Young Minds.* Chatsworth, Calif.: Datamost, 1984. Reprinted in *The Computing Teacher* 12 (May 1985): 8–9.

Clark, Richard E. "Computers Can't Teach." *The Institute* (the newspaper of IEEE) 9 (January 1985): 5.

Ferguson, Marilyn. *The Aquarian Conspiracy: Personal and Social Transformation in the 1980s.* Los Angeles: J. P. Tarcher, 1980.

Graves, Donald H., and Virginia Stuart. *Write from the Start: Tapping Your Child's Natural Ability.* New York: E. P. Dutton, 1985.

Murray, Donald. *Write to Learn.* New York: Holt, 1984.

"Personal Computer in a Writing Course." *Perspectives in Computing.* Vol. 4, No. 1 (Spring 1984): 6.

Rico, Gabriele. *Writing the Natural Way: Using the Right Brain to Release Your Expressive Powers.* Boston: Houghton Mifflin, 1983.

Schwartz, Helen. *Interactive Writing.* New York: Holt, 1985.

Turkle, Sherry. *The Second Self: Computers and the Human Spirit.* New York: Simon and Schuster, 1984.

ACKNOWLEDGMENTS

I am indebted to Dr. Said M. Hamdan for the original impetus to undertake teaching the technical writing class with a computer lab. Dr. Bernard Sagik encouraged me to seek support from the Fund for the Improvement of Post-Secondary Education, and Dr. Stephen Ehrmann of the Fund guided my efforts at evaluating the project. Professors Bernard Brenner, Judith Scheffler, and Gisele Bathish have been indefatigable readers and commenters on early forms of this essay. Most important, I am grateful to the hundreds of students who shared my enthusiasm for a new idea and who taught me how to use a computer in the process of discovering why to use it.

An Ethnographic Study of a High School Writing Class Using Computers

Marginal, Technically Proficient, and Productive Learners

ANDREA W. HERRMANN

During the 1983–1984 academic year, I introduced the word processor into my high school writing class of eight students. I designed the course around it to permit the close observation of students, and I studied my class using ethnographic techniques: videotape, audiotape, teacher/researcher journals, student journals, students' writing, and interviews. Ethnographic research encourages us to look at classroom behaviors in relation to the larger educational context in order to generate hypotheses—new lenses through which future learning situations can be viewed and may be more clearly understood. Observing the participants' patterns of behavior in their relationships to each other and to the tasks at hand stimulates speculation about the nature of this behavior and about the effects of this social interaction on the learning process.

Kathleen Wilcox points out that educational ethnographers frequently view school as the agent of cultural transmission. What goes on in classrooms reflects the larger society ("Ethnography as a Methodology," 463). Ethnographic studies portray American classrooms as places where student performance is constantly evaluated; where students are taught, in addition to the formal curriculum, an informal one that includes values, self-images, motivational strategies, and relationships to peers and authority figures; and where students are stratified by differential expectations based on social class.

Educators often view their roles as promoting opportunity, reform, and change ("Ethnography as a Methodology," 463). This was essentially my view of things as I introduced the computer into my classroom. I hoped it would provide my students with new opportunities to develop as writers, perhaps even as readers and thinkers.

Yet, as Wilcox says, problems arise in introducing educational change. Ethnographic studies show that efforts at instituting reform may come up against *"strong continuities with past arrangements"* ("Ethnography as a Methodology," 469; my emphasis). In the unfolding of events in my classroom, some things differed from conventional high school writing classes, whereas other things remained essentially the same. My analysis of the data suggests that three types of learners emerged: marginal learners, those who had protracted problems learning how to use the word processor and who made little progress in their writing; technically proficient learners, those who became adept at word processing but who made little writing progress; and productive learners, those who were successful on both fronts. I look here at the the social dynamics in my classroom and at the relationship between the teaching and learning styles. And on the basis of my understanding of what took place, I suggest pedagogical approaches to facilitate teaching composition with the computer.

CHANGES AND CONTINUITIES: THE CLASSROOM CONTEXT

Class Composition

Because of the in-depth nature of the research, I restricted class size to eight students. They were sophomores, juniors, and seniors from the various tracking levels (the lowest level up to gifted students and advanced-placement students). Such integration was a significant change for students at this school (it resulted not from the research design but from the principal's requirement that only students with third-period study hall be allowed to volunteer for the class).

Teaching Methodology

One obvious change from traditional classes was the unconventional design of the course. Students were asked to spend their time on writing-related activities, either on or off the computer, to maintain a daily writing-process journal outside of class, and to do their best. There were no assignments (initially), no deadlines, and no minimum amount of writing required. The class was less rigidly structured and the teaching style less teacher-centered than that of conventional high school classes. Because there were few goals and expectations set forth in the course, I thought that students would find this learning environment appealing. I failed to take into consideration, however, that because the course goals were not defined, many of my expectations were implicit rather than explicit. Students lacked the usual course guidelines to measure themselves, and as a result, their tasks as learners might be viewed as more complex rather than as simplified.

Another change from convention was that I was researching the class. In addition to the face-to-face interactions between teacher and student that might be expected in a class of this nature (for example, the teacher sitting with students at the computer to discuss their writing), there was a constant ongoing evaluation—not via tests or graded papers, but in the form of teacher/researcher activities: close and prolonged observations including note taking, videotaping, and interviewing. Students might be considered to have been overly attended to at times. On the other hand, acting as researcher also made me less available to students sometimes. At the start of the year, for example, students needed much help, but research helpers and equipment needed special attention, too.

There were continuities as well. I was an English teacher of long standing in the school at the time of the study, the class took place in a classroom during the school day, and the students took the course for academic credit.

Teaching Equipment

The course centered on learning how to write using microcomputers as word processors. We used Apple II Plus and IIe computers and the "Bank Street Writer" word processing program. Although some students had had a little exposure to computers (mostly to play games), none had ever used a word processor before.

EXPLICIT AND IMPLICIT EXPECTATIONS

Although these conditions imposed new demands on students, these demands arose within the context of the normal expectations of the school setting. This was still "school," both in the students' minds and in mine. Because most people do not have access to their most fundamental assumptions, I was often unaware of my own. Based on the students' responses, however, I became aware of some of my implicit expectations as well as those inherent in the nature of the course. Whether expectations at any given moment in the year were explicit or implicit for students shifted like the ebb and flow of the tides. The following list of expectations is incomplete, but it represents the kinds of demands, implicit as well as explicit, that this course made on students. Students were expected

1. To be able to learn primarily through demonstration, interaction with the computer program through trial and error, and problem-solving strategies rather than via a more structured, segmented, and graded sequence of instructional activities presented by the teacher.
2. To be able to admit to themselves and to others when difficulties arose and to seek assistance from classmates or the teacher when necessary.
3. To be willing to help other classmates or the teacher, as the need arose or when asked.
4. To be willing to expose their learning processes in using the computer equipment and in learning to write; to be willing to make available their writing while it was still in process, not only when they felt it was a finished product.
5. To be able to discover and initiate for themselves learning activities that related to writing and had meaning for them as learners.
6. To be able to tolerate ambiguity and uncertainty, especially regarding the idiosyncrasies of the new technology; to be flexible and adaptable learners who could adjust to the unforeseen (roll with the electronic punches, so to speak).
7. To be able to tolerate a teaching situation in which the teacher would not always know, or even pretend to know, all the answers; to work with a teacher who expected to solve problems along with the students.
8. To be willing to attempt to solve problems, their own or their classmates', by themselves or with the help of others, as these problems arose within the class.
9. To be able to acknowledge their accomplishments and to take pride in them.
10. To be able to maintain interest in their work and gain momentum for continuing it because of their own personal response to it rather than in pursuit of a grade.

11. To be able to distinguish "writing" activities from "word processing" activities and to be willing to shift their involvement from word processing to writing as time went on.
12. To be able to see the value of writing, or to learn to value it, as a meaningful personal activity.

INTERNAL VERSUS EXTERNAL GOALS

These expectations led to an environment that differed from that of the traditional classroom. It demanded from students a greater degree of independence, self-reliance, and inner control in order to direct their behavior toward course goals. Paradoxically, it also demanded interdependence, the ability to work one-on-one with peers and with the teacher. The learning situation shifted from the more usual teacher-dominated classroom, with tasks and information meted out according to some preestablished sequence for a predetermined reward or punishment (grade), to a more egalitarian, student-centered classroom, with students expected to take primary responsibility for initiating activities and for assessing their value in learning to work with a word processor and to write.

Although students were in charge of their own learning, they were not free to do whatever they wished. I had defined the overall course goals. Students were free only to the extent that they had internalized these explicit goals and could regulate their activities and behavior in accordance with them. Initially, the course had few built-in, externally controlled mechanisms. As time went on, however, I built in more external structure in the form of periodic, teacher-created writing assignments with deadlines. I also assumed the role of disciplinarian. I interceded when in my estimation students' behavior did not conform to course expectations (were not writing or doing writing-related work), impeded others in the room, or violated school rules.

My basic assumption, so fundamental that it remained largely unexamined throughout a good deal of the study, was that students would enjoy working in a setting offering these new freedoms. Therefore, I did not at first make important connections between the environment and the mounting evidence that some students were not doing well.

STUDENT BEHAVIOR PATTERNS

How did students respond to the expectation that they would internalize academic and behavioral standards? The most noticeable reaction was that this experience dichotomized them—not once, but twice. In the beginning the group divided sharply into those who learned how to use the word processor quickly and those who did not. Later, students polarized into those who became engaged by writing and those who did not.

The marginal students appeared overwhelmed and confused. They found it difficult to learn to use the word processor and to write in this environment. Their conduct was frequently inappropriate, both academically and behaviorally. The productive learners thrived in this atmosphere; they said they liked the freedom of having no assignments and deadlines. This experience invigorated them and gave them a new enthusiasm for learning and for writing. They discovered effective ways to learn, and they liked what they were doing. They managed their behavior appropriately. The technically proficient learners flourished in the beginning, learning word processing successfully, only to fade in the end, engaging in little writing.

In other words, the computer, the teacher's and student's enthusiasm, the innovative course—none of these worked a learning miracle in my class. There were in fact "strong continuities with past arrangements." Introducing the computer into this context appeared to do little to improve the status quo for the students who traditionally do not do well in school.

I believe that the new demands made by the computer and the course design, along with the research process and the mixed-ability tracks, exacerbated the class divisions made by the larger society and mirrored by the school. The hierarchical stratification of students by academic track for the most part prevailed. Most students who were accustomed to experiencing alienation in school, who saw themselves as failures, "failed"; most students who were accustomed to getting by "got by"; and the students who were accustomed to doing well "did well."

But this is a schematic view. It leaves out important details. One student, Chad, who according to expectation should have been one to "get by," in fact "did well." Another student, Carmen, who appeared destined to "fail," persisted until the end of the year and "got by." The students fated to "do well" did more than just "well." They overcame blocks and anxieties and became highly engaged in their writing. Even the students who "failed," in my opinion, did not fail. They changed and grew in some important ways. They came up against an exceedingly difficult situation for them, struggled, and learned a good deal about working with people and about themselves as learners. They also learned more about computers and writing.

Although many factors were at work, an important ingredient in students' eventual success in the course was whether they perceived themselves as successful learners. The students had learned their past lessons well. They knew their place in the social order of things and their place in the educational tracking system. They came into this new learning context expecting to take their accustomed place there as well. But they faced strong ambivalences. The lower-track students in particular didn't want to be at the bottom of the hierarchy, and I didn't want them to be there either. Together they and I hoped the computer could provide a new way.

But instead of making things easier, the computer sometimes made things harder. At times we were engaged in a trying, human struggle. We couldn't always communicate effectively. There wasn't always enough trust or good will or optimism when it was needed. Although I did not fully understand what was happening at the time, I have come to believe that we were struggling against one of the most entrenched features of our culture, social class.

AN EXPLANATION: DIFFERENTIAL SOCIALIZATION

Ethnographic research suggests that children are socialized both in society and at school according to their class background (Wilcox, "Differential Socialization," 271). Melvin Kohn and others indicate that workers at lower levels are directed by structures external to themselves: rules, routines, and regulations ("Differential Socialization," 273–274). Workers at higher professional levels, however, are expected to be directed by structures internal to themselves: motivation and judgment corresponding to the needs of the organization but so internalized by the individual that they are produced independently, without the obvious external constraints. Wilcox, in her research on two first-grade classrooms, one in a lower-middle-class school and one in an upper-middle-class school, concludes that the teachers, the principal, the school district, and even the state participated in creating an environment where students were differentially socialized for their future positions in the world of work on the basis of the school personnel's perceptions of their parents' class level ("Differential Socialization," 269–309).

In the upper-middle-class schoolroom, the children in Wilcox's study learned skills, values, and attitudes in preparation for professional roles. They received encouragement, they were taught to think of their present actions as having future consequences, and they learned to internalize both academic and behavioral standards ("Differential Socialization," 289–294). In the lower-middle-class schoolroom, the children were allowed to do more activities just for fun; they were given a greater latitude to be simply kids. They focused on the present rather than on the future. They were *not* expected to behave in more mature ways in anticipation of future demands, and they were disciplined by the external sanctions of higher authority—the rules and regulations of teacher and school ("Differential Socialization," 291–295).

If Wilcox's research captures the essence of the differential treatment generally given to students in lower-track classrooms versus higher-track classrooms—as I believe it does—it seems likely that one reason my students from the lower tracks had difficulty learning was the lack of correspondence between the teaching style they were accustomed to and the style I was using. My course design and teaching manner essentially demanded that students internalize the course goals, especially the implicit notion that they were to be independent, self-directed learners and writers. Rather than imposing an explicit, authoritarian, rule-sanctioned structure, I created an environment that inadvertently assumed students were socialized to an upper-middle-class value system—one likely to be at odds with the educational experiences and expectations of some students, perhaps even with the interactional dynamics in their homes. In expecting that students could internalize the course standards academically and behaviorally, I had unwittingly created a situation of unequal opportunity that gave upper-track students a distinct advantage.

Some students had been prepared by school, possibly even by their families, for many of the implicit expectations and demands inherent in my course design and teaching style: the upper-middle-class values of internalizing the goals of the work place. Accustomed to taking responsibility and initiative for their development as learners, they were comfortable with and ready to meet the challenges of this class.

They worked effectively within it. Others' prior school experiences had taught them an essentially opposite, even contradictory, position. They had learned to work within a more externally motivated system characterized by explicit rules, rewards, and punishments and oriented to the here-and-now rather than the distant future. Used to being told what to do and when to do it, these students were not able to make sense of my class with all its supposed freedoms.

Marginal Learners

In addition to my teaching style and expectations, other factors kept some students from feeling at home in this environment and positive about their learning. The mixing of tracks placed those accustomed to being at the bottom of the academic hierarchy, the marginal learners, into face-to-face competition, at least in their minds, with the students who "outranked them" in the socioeconomic status of the larger society and in the school tracking system.

I attempted to minimize competition in the class by eliminating tests and grades and by telling students not to worry about how fast someone else was learning. Yet the students, conditioned to compare themselves with others, continued to compete. In fact the computer, with its public display of writing, contributed to this competitive effect. It broadcast the struggles of some at the same time that it heralded the success of others. I undoubtedly contributed also, though I tried not to. Students noticed, for example, whose journals or parts of papers I read as examples of good writing. Some apparently believed that the cards were stacked against them in this competition, and they perceived the others as intimidating. Those who were used to losing out in the academic arena found it difficult to ask for help from me or the other students, especially those students they perceived to be ahead of them.

The small class size and the research activities also appeared to heighten their difficulties—there was no place to hide. I constantly observed and wrote things down; the video assistant was continually taping them as they worked. It must have seemed to some that they got caught every time they did something wrong. I told students that the only way they could progress was to make mistakes and to learn from them. But for some students, making mistakes was demoralizing. They believed the research was really a trap meant to catch them, to show that they couldn't learn after all. Their reading difficulties and their problems following directions were exacerbated by their beliefs about not being smart, about not fitting into this class, about not belonging. All of these factors worked to create so much anxiety that some students' ability to function became seriously impaired.

It appeared to be hard for these marginal learners to concentrate and to figure things out. They believed they were not getting enough help from me, even when I thought they were getting a good deal of it. They may have been trying to communicate (but could not articulate) that I was not giving them the right *kind* of help. I was not giving them a highly structured course with material presented in small digestible bits, the type of sequential teaching they may have been most familiar with.

They came up with strategies to avoid the punishing confrontation with the computer and with the class, but the more successful they became at avoidance, the less contact they had with the computer and the less opportunity they had to learn. This spiraling situation meant that some students fell farther and farther behind the others in the class competition, reinforcing the marginal learners' fears that they were not smart enough to learn how to use the computer.

Technically Proficient Learners

The success of the technically proficient learners with word processing *but their avoidance of writing* may result from a similar lack of fit—one less serious than that for marginal learners—between their experiences as learners and the demands of the learning environment. Their existing skills and abilities were more highly developed. They were better readers and writers, and they gave evidence of having more self-confidence in coping with this class. Their perceptions of themselves as learners seemed hardier, less vulnerable to assaults made by the process of learning to use the computer.

The technically proficient learners apparently had little trouble with the course expectations for the more mechanical and practical activities of learning word processing. They appeared to have internalized the necessary behavioral standards. Once the focus of the course shifted to writing, however, difficulties began to develop. These students did not display the same willingness to expose their writing as they had their word processing skills.

The process of differential socialization that Wilcox describes for the lower-middle and the upper-middle classes may have an intermediate category. That is, the school may socialize certain students to fit into the requirements for middle-middle-class jobs. If so, these students might be expected to be socialized to fill some occupational niche mid-way between the laborer, who is supposed to accept the direction of an external authority, and the full professional, who is expected to show independent judgment. Such students—like my technically proficient learners—might be socialized to accept the external direction of authority at times, yet still to operate according to internalized values and motivation when the demands made on them suited the values that they have been socialized to. Whereas socialization for the upper-middle-class jobs would prepare students for work in highly autonomous professional positions—as doctors or lawyers, for example—socialization for middle-middle-class jobs would prepare them for work in semi-autonomous positions in structured settings—as laboratory technicians, perhaps, or legal secretaries.

PEDAGOGICAL IMPLICATIONS

What does all this suggest for writing teachers who use word processing in their classes? The most obvious conclusion is that the computer's presence in our classrooms appears unlikely to negate the powerful influence of the differential socialization of students by social class and its effects on their success or failure in school. The computer's revolutionary impact on literacy, if it comes, will probably not come effortlessly or easily. It may in fact require the restructuring of our current educational system, if we expect all students to reap the potential benefits. My study suggests that simply placing computers within the existing structure of classroom and school, even in a classroom of highly motivated students and teacher, is unlikely to promote equal learning opportunities for all.

But I am not pessimistic about the value of the computer as a writing tool in the classroom. There are real benefits currently—and even greater potential benefits down the road—for all students, even those who traditionally do not do well in school. Some options are already possible, and others will soon be available: word processing programs that are easier to learn; more integrated software permitting students to work with a variety of on-line prewriting, drafting, and editing programs; and networked computers that increase software access, foster collaboration, and allow information gathering via data bases.

Although macro-level changes probably must occur for equality to become an educational reality, some lower-level modifications in the educational approach are now within the teacher's control: teachers can increase the possibility of success for all students by using the computer as a writing tool.

Teaching Word Processing

One way to successfully reach various types of learners would be to separate the teaching of word processing from the teaching of writing in the early stages of word processing instruction. Such a division would clarify for both teacher and students the central purpose of the teaching/learning activities. This clarity may be lacking in a course that attempts to do both at the same time. Presumably, such a division would also reduce the "overload" experienced by some students as they write, when they haven't become competent in operating the word processing program. Writing is difficult enough for many students without adding the complications of half-understood word processing procedures. Such a division would encourage the development of pedagogical strategies and tasks necessary to teach word processing skills, rather than relegating such an important activity to *ad hoc* or *post hoc* measures.

At the core of this suggestion is the notion that word processing skills should become somewhat automatic before too much composing is expected of students. Then the writer is free to concentrate on composing, itself a complex mental process. Just as the novice pianist plays simple tunes until she achieves greater dexterity and familiarity with the piano, the novice at word processing should begin by manipulating small pieces of text that are inconsequential to her—pieces that she herself has not written—at least until she achieves a modicum of comfort and competence with the program's procedures. Much like a course in personal typing, this course would emphasize word processing skills needed by a writer rather than a secretary. A word processing class for writers would not use the same syllabus or even the same word processing program as one for secretaries, because the needs of the two groups are quite different.

Programs for business are not always compatible with the writing process. Designed for people who copy documents, they are not necessarily good for writers composing directly at the keyboard. Automatic mechanisms that interfere with composing force the writer to interrupt himself—perhaps as he struggles to capture the essence of a still-forming thought—and deal with mechanical matters such as where to hyphenate a word. This seriously disrupts the formation and flow of ideas. While sometimes the user can disable these devices to prevent them from intruding, it is obviously preferable for writers to use programs free from such obstacles. Writers need software that attends to their special needs—that permits, for example, the automatic formating and placement of footnotes, the splitting of the screen so that the writer can work on two parts of the same document side by side, and the windowing of one document into another for simultaneous access to both.

Writers also need to be taught the commands essential to composing and revising at the keyboard, particularly those for deleting, inserting, and moving text. They need to learn how to manipulate files; how to format compositions, poems, and term papers; and how to print out their papers. Without courses emphasizing the writer's special needs, much of the power of word processing may remain untapped by the writer.

This course should be taught by the English department rather than the business department. A writing teacher is more likely to serve the writer's needs than a business teacher. The process of updating software and (if necessary) replacing hardware may be hopelessly complicated when the teaching is in the hands of another department. New and improved versions of software and hardware quickly outdate previous ones, yet change is complicated by the lack of standardization and by incompatibility between programs and equipment. Expecting business teachers to understand the requirements of English teachers and to meet their needs is unrealistic.

If a separate course cannot be implemented, the writing teacher might teach word processing and writing in the same course, but not at the same time—at least not in the early phases of the class. This separation would improve the quality of word processing instruction and encourage students to use the most common commands and procedures until they felt a degree of confidence before creating their own texts. Confidence at the computer should also minimize students' anxiety about losing their writing.

Assessing Teaching Style

However, the ideal course for students must do more than separate the early phases of word processing from composition. Teachers should become sensitive to the social dynamics in their classrooms and to the compatibility of their teaching style with the learning styles of their students. As my findings suggest, when there is a lack of fit, the students' ability to learn may suffer. In my class, some students appeared to be more comfortable with a teaching structure external to themselves, with the course rules and expectations explicitly delineated. Yet there were others who responded more positively to greater self-direction and freedom. They learned well and were happier when they were allowed more autonomy. They benefited from the freedom to initiate their own learning activities and to complete them at their own speed. The teacher's dilemma is to create a course that satisfies the wide range of these needs.

To make meaningful changes, the teacher must first evaluate her teaching practices. Is she a teacher who likes a highly structured course or a loosely structured one? Does she use primarily external writing motivation (tests, grades, and so forth) or internal motivation encouraging students to write for self and peers? And is her classroom essentially teacher-dominated or essentially student-centered?

After the teacher gets some perspective on her teaching style (which is no doubt related to her own preferences as a learner), she needs to discover those of her students and then attempt to modify her techniques accordingly. This may sound impossible for the busy classroom teacher to do, especially if the students in the class—like mine—represent a range of styles. Yet the obstacles may not be insurmountable. Rather than attempting to change her teaching style to accommodate each learner's preference, the teacher needs to provide a structure loose enough for students who benefit from autonomy, yet tight enough for those who prefer to work within explicit guidelines. In addition, rather than changing her style completely to suit her students, the teacher may create transitional activities designed to help students gradually adjust to her teaching style. Although the outcome of introducing change is always unpredictable, such a course might allow a greater number of students to succeed.

My study suggests that some students in my class might have benefited from more structure than I provided, both in the word processing and in the writing instruction. However, word processing is not a linear activity learned through doing a sequential series of discrete tasks. Learning word processing, like learning other complex computer skills such as programming, requires a good deal of user exploration and interaction with the program. Students must be willing to learn through trial and error. This study has taught me one of the most important things we have to teach our writers: Mastery of a word processing program requires a willingness to interact, to explore, and to experiment. Students need to learn (and teachers have to communicate) that there is no such thing as a mistake, that computer learning entails error, and that almost anything that goes awry can be fixed.

Structuring the Course

It might appear that this need for students to learn through trial and error precludes the use of structured activities in the classroom. However, both types of activities are helpful. In an effort to show how I would integrate the theoretical aspects of my findings into the day-to-day world of my teaching practices, I will describe how I would teach a similar course now. I am assuming I would be teaching a combined course in word processing and writing, keeping the two separate during the early stages of word processing.

A class size of 14 to 20 students would be ideal. Large enough to permit students to work in groups and learn from each other, it would be small enough for students to receive individual help regularly from me. A ratio of two students to each computer would be fine, at least in the beginning. Once the focus of the course shifted from acquiring basic word processing skills to independent writing, it would be better to have one student per computer.

I would actively foster collaborative activities in my class, requiring students to work in pairs while learning the basics of word processing and encouraging students to assist each other freely. Assuming I needed to give grades, I would also grade these collaborative activities. Student pairs would work through a learning packet of word processing activities at their own pace but would be required to meet periodic deadlines. The tasks would be in electronic files copied onto students' disks as well as on paper for the student to key in. Only one activity for each section would be required, because all activities within a section would be designed to teach the same group of skills. But, of course, students would be able to do more if they wanted practice. Those who worked quickly would be encouraged to design their own learning exercises, using skills they had acquired. I would do demonstrations and help students who were having problems.

No original writing would be expected at first, but if some students wanted to perform the required word processing skills on their own writing, they could do so. Activities would start with short, simple, mechanical tasks. A first activity might consist of the student booting in a disk, calling up a file, changing something within it, and saving it. The student might, for example, have to change all of the first letters of each sentence in a paragraph from lower-case letters to capitals. Other activities could require a student to do a search to eliminate a redundant word, to find and replace a misspelled word, to move sentences in a paragraph into a new order, or to move paragraphs into a different sequence to make a text read more coherently. The nature and sequence of activities would be based on the particular word processing program; some things that are relatively simple to do in one program are more complex in another.

Some of these tasks would require the input of text—for example, a cloze exercise, which consists of a paragraph with periodic blanks to be filled in. Although some tasks would be more language-focused and less mechanical, the goal would still be learning the appropriate word processing strategies; the quality of the student's use of language would not be evaluated. Original writing could be encouraged by asking students to compose two silly sentences, respond to a series of humorous questions, complete a series of half-written metaphors, and so forth. Gradually more complex word processing skills would be required. For some students this phase of the course might take only two or three weeks. For others it might take longer.

When the emphasis of the course shifted to writing, I would continue to encourage students to work collaboratively. I would structure assignments loosely and set deadlines. A student selection of revised pieces would be evaluated for the semester grade. As I had done in the word processing phase, I would strive to create sufficient structure to guide students in working productively and to allow enough freedom to motivate those who prefer greater autonomy. Some assignments would permit students to select their topic from within prescribed boundaries—for example, to write a review of an event, work of art, or production. Other assignments would be more narrowly focused while providing for a choice among several options.

If there were, for example, fifteen units in a learning packet (such as poetry, a character description, a persuasive essay, a review, etc.), students might be required to do a total of twelve projects: ten selected from the fifteen sections in the packet, and two of their own creation. Those who had difficulty coming up with writing ideas of their own could complete twelve projects from the packet. Although there would be regular deadlines, the students could hand in assignments in any order they chose. Special permission could be negotiated for students engaged in long or cooperative projects to have them count as two or more assignments. In this manner, I would hope to provide sufficient direction for those students who especially require structure, while at the same time encouraging self-direction in students who thrive on freedom.

Introducing educational change, like tampering with habitats in nature, entails the willingness to deal with unpredictable results, because "strong continuities with past arrangements" exist. Yet the potential for improving the educational opportunities for all our students makes taking the risks worthwhile. Appropriately designed and implemented, courses in using the computer as a writing tool have the potential to make greater numbers of students into more skillful writers.

REFERENCES

Wilcox, Kathleen. "Differential Socialization in the Classroom: Implications for Equal Opportunity." In *Doing the Ethnography of Schooling: Educational Anthropology in Action*, edited by George Spindler. New York: CBS College Publishing, 1982, pp. 269–309.

————. "Ethnography as a Methodology and Its Application to the Study of Schooling: A Review." In *Doing the Ethnography of Schooling: Educational Anthropology in Action*, edited by George Spindler. New York: CBS College Publishing, 1982, pp. 456–488.

PART TWO

THEORETICAL AND POLITICAL ISSUES

Some Ideas About Idea Processors

DAVID N. DOBRIN

To put it simply, "idea processors" are computer programs that can relieve us of some of the annoyances associated with making outlines. When we outline with pencil and paper, if we want to make the outline go more than three or four levels deep, we run out of room on the page, and if we want to emend or move items, the marks that are already there get in the way. When we outline with a word processor we can keep our copy clean, but there isn't much room on the screen, so we can't go very deep there, either. Indentation on word processors, moreover, is a little tricky, and changing indentation levels or moving blocks is usually clumsy, particularly because all the levels of headings must be updated. "Idea processors" get around all these problems. A user can move, reorder, renumber, expand on, or delete entries with the push of a button.

These programs raise the same problems for writing teachers that word processors did a few years ago. Are the programs useful? If so, how useful are they? Should we offer them to students? Should their use be taught? In the rest of this article, I will try to provide some answers to these questions. The answers, let me say in advance, are a bit deflating: I will argue that idea processors are not particularly useful for most people, that students don't need them and might even need to be steered away from them, and that teachers should certainly not include them in the curriculum.

Any casual observer will find that my conclusions run counter to what one may intuitively feel about idea processors. Planning, after all, is an important part of the writing process; outlining is frequently a useful step in planning; and therefore anything that helps people outline should be valuable. (Many people apparently find this logic so persuasive that they have invested in outlining programs; as I write this [October 1985], "ThinkTank," the most popular of them, is seventh on the word processing best-seller list.) Less casual observers, like the people who have developed these programs or the people who market them, might well find my conclusions ridiculous. Naturally the developers are enthusiastic about their programs, which they see as a major advance in computerized writing aids. They seldom characterize the programs as outlining aids; rather, the programs are presented as "aids to thinking." The designers of these programs give them names like "ThinkTank" and "MaxThink"; they use the generic term *idea processor* without quotation marks or even any indication that quotation marks are necessary. (I contend that the quotation marks *are* necessary, for, as I will show, ideas are not what these programs actually process.)

On the face of it, the developers' enthusiasm is not completely implausible. When you plan a paper with an outline, you must generate ideas, assess their importance, and place them in suitable order. Idea processors *do* help you order ideas, designate their importance, and thus, in this limited way, help you think. But these programs *don't* help you think in an expansive way. By helping you to manipulate symbols, they restrict your creativity to words you've already put on paper. Expansive thinking—*true* idea processing—occurs in the mind, not on paper. It engages the mind's full creative possibilities. If you want to manipulate ideas, help with manipulating symbols is largely beside the point.

The interesting question, and the one that will be my primary focus in the following section, is *why* manipulating symbols is beside the point. To answer that question, I will have to range over some decidedly disparate subjects, including notions of creativity and the idea that there might be something like a method for writing. Because most current theories of the writing process (such as those propounded by Flower and Hayes [1981]) suggest that there is something like a method, I will not only disagree with the makers of these programs but also attack those theories. In the main, though, I take a practical rather than a theoretical approach. I'll look carefully at the programs and try to give you an intuitive feeling for what goes wrong when you make symbol manipulation substitute for thinking. Essentially, even though idea processors save you the work of updating symbols (headings and subheadings, for instance), you still have to update the ideas. If you don't, the fact that the updated symbols no longer correctly indicate the updated ideas makes the new outline too confusing to be useful. To use idea processors effectively, you would have to spend a lot of time learning how to cope with the confusing lists of items that these programs help you produce. And, except for people deeply committed to outlines, the time spent isn't worth it.

THE CLAIMS FOR IDEA PROCESSORS

The idea processor I've used is a program called "MaxThink." (Its capabilities are listed in Tables 9.1, 9.2, 9.3.)

"MaxThink" was developed by a very energetic man named Neil Larson. Larson writes his own promotional materials and manuals, so to tell you more about his program (and, by extension, all others), I can simply quote him. According to

Table 9.1.   "MaxThink" Text Manipulation Commands

Add Title	Begins new outine
Insert Topic	Inserts heading or subheading before or after current entry
Delete	Words or Letters
Insert Word	In current entry
Annotate	Inserts comments after entry
Jump	Moves cursor to specified path number, such as 1.1.3.4, allowing you to zoom in on any section of the outline
Move	Moves any item or group of items to a new area of the outline
Search and Replace	Like word processing

Table 9.2. "MaxThink" File Manipulation Commands

DOS File Manipulation	Renames, copies, or deletes files
Insert File	Inserts a file in an outline
Print	Prints a file (multiple options)
View	Views a DOS file
Save	Saves your file

Larson, the "idea processor" or "thought processor" is a "radical departure" from a word processor or spreadsheet because it can "interact directly with the higher-level thinking skills" and thus "improve the productivity of your thoughts" (P 1, 3, 1).[1] The thought processing commands "support high-level thinking" (P 3), "expand your writing and thinking abilities," and "improve your insight, perception, imagination, and creative thinking" (P 2). The program is, in short, "mind-expanding software" (M 3).

But these claims are true of virtually any tool; I would probably grant a carpenter's claim that a T-square is in some sense "mind-expanding" and "thought-supporting," insofar as it helps him plan his work. But Larson means something stronger than this. For him, the program literally takes over some of the thinking jobs for you: "MaxThink provides the system, structures, and commands for pondering, discovering, expanding, and integrating information" (P 3).

One might, of course, make this stronger claim for any tool that performs algorithmic processes. A calculator expands your adding capabilities and supports additive thinking by taking over some of the adding for you. Without a calculator, you must enter numbers on a sheet of paper, add them, and enter the result. With a calculator, you only enter the numbers; the calculator adds and enters the result. Similarly, an idea processor like "MaxThink" might help you prioritize by taking the phrases you enter and placing them in a hierarchy. Unfortunately, though, the similarity is misleading. It confuses labels or symbols (which are on paper or in the computer) with ideas (which are in the head). A priority is an idea; a phrase with a number (such as 1) attached to it is a symbol that stands for the idea of priority. When an idea processor "prioritizes," it does not set priorities: It attaches labels indicating priorities that the writer has set. This confusion between symbol and idea underlies all the false claims about idea processors.

The confusion, by the way, is inherent in my earlier description of how calculators work. Calculators do not manipulate numbers, which are meaningful; they manipulate symbols for numbers. Strictly speaking, calculators don't even add; they simulate adding. Calculators simulate adding successfully because (for numerical calculations) we have worked out mechanical processes that manipulate numbers. So the confusion doesn't matter; it makes sense to speak of the calculator as adding because the calculator performs a process that is formally similar to addition.

If we could work out similar mechanical processes for prioritization, then, again, the confusion would not matter; we could sensibly speak of a prioritizer as

[1] I am quoting from the promotional material for "MaxThink" (P), from the *MaxThink Newsletter* (N), and from the MaxThink manual (M). All are published by the MaxThink Corporation of Piedmont, California; all are circa 1984. References for the quotations will give the letter and page number, where pages are numbered.

Table 9.3. Special MaxThink Commands ("MaxThink" also has a LISP-like "Thought Processing Language," which allows you to program the use of these commands.)

Prioritize	Renumbers entries
Binsort	Puts entries into different "bins"
Levelize	Removes hierarchical distinctions "Fence"
	Allows you to label groups of entries
Join	Joins entries
Divide	Separates entries
Randomize	Relabels entries randomly
Sort	Sorts entries in alphabetical (or other) order
Tag	Provides a space for tags, which can then be used in sorting

taking over some of our prioritizing processes for us. But no such mechanical prioritization processes have been worked out, nor are they likely to be.[2] And, in any case, idea processors do not implement such a process.

In sum, idea processors process not ideas but symbols; therefore they don't support thinking processes any more than word processors or T-squares do. Why then do people like Larson make such claims or (worse yet) believe them? I think that they allow themselves to be confused by the difference between ideas and symbols because they make three, quite different assumptions.

1. Thinking is fundamentally algorithmic (and thus, according to Church's and Turing's thesis, it can be simulated by a mechanical process). This assumption has been accepted as obviously true in our culture ever since Plato.[3] This assumption does not, as I have pointed out, mean anything when it comes to idea processors, because they don't incorporate a mechanical process that simulates thinking. But this assumption can lead to the mistaken belief that, if an algorithmic process *facilitates* thinking, it is therefore a tool *expressly designed* for thinking—that the process works in the same way thinking works. That's why it's easier to consider a calculator a thinking tool than to consider a T-square a thinking tool: A calculator facilitates thinking more than a T-square does. The mistake (confusing facilitating with simulating) is commonly made. The programming ideas used in "MaxThink," for example, are based on programming ideas incorporated in LISP, a language developed for artificial-intelligence applications. In the artificial intelligence community, LISP implementations are commonly spoken of as just such special aids to thinking. Indeed, according to one LISP instructor at M.I.T., LISP is the language that "lets a computer think."

2. Meanings are on the page, so manipulating the symbols is manipulating the meanings. Again, there's powerful support for this idea. Philosophers routinely argue that meanings are not in the head (Putnam). Most branches of linguistics assume that there is a distinction between the meaning of a word and its use and

---

[2] See my "Limitations on the Use of Computers in Writing and the Teaching of Writing" in *The Future of Computers in Composition*, forthcoming. For a full discussion of the limitations of computers, see Hubert L. Dreyfus, *What Computers Can't Do*.

[3] For more on this, see Dreyfus, *op. cit.*, and also *Putting Computers in Their Proper Place*, forthcoming.

that the literal meaning is independent of the use.[4] This assumption does not, of course, mean that any manipulation of symbols is a manipulation of their meaning, because many manipulations of symbols (such as rearranging the letters in a word) don't preserve the meaning through the manipulations. On this assumption, a symbol manipulator can be a meaning manipulator only if it is what John Haugeland calls "a semantic engine"—that is, if it preserves the meaning during each operation. There is no reason to believe that idea processors are "semantic engines." But many people believe it is possible to build a machine that manipulates symbols according to more powerful semantic and syntactic rules and which would then literally help us write. And idea processors might well be the first step on the way.

3. The best method of writing is to make an outline of the paper to be written and then expand the outline's entries indefinitely. If you believe this, you should use idea processors whether or not you believe the other assumptions, because they make this method of writing (apparently) easier. Those who accept this assumption, surely, are those who are making "ThinkTank" into a best-seller.

Combine these three assumptions, add a pinch of confusion and a tablespoon of belief that your livelihood is on the line, and you can see why the developers believe that their idea processors are accurately named. Add for dessert the belief that "most mental processes simply amount to picking the best option from a group of many choices" (P 3), and you can get up from the table thinking that idea processors ought to be on everyone's desk.

If you don't believe these assumptions, however, the programs suddenly don't look so appetizing. The question then becomes "How good are they really?" In the next section, I want to address that question.

HOW USEFUL ARE IDEA PROCESSORS?

If idea processors only manipulate symbols for ideas, allowing one to group the symbols, to expand on them, to reorder them, to put them into hierarchies, and (alas) to erase them, then are idea processors useful for planning, noodling, brainstorming, or "shifting perceptions," as the makers claim? Are they as useful for writing as those who believe the last assumption apparently feel? And if so, how?

The answer is complicated, because any tool can be useful if you are committed to using it for some purpose and want to take the time to learn how to use it. (You could probably, eventually, cut diamonds with a backhoe.) So I'm not going to claim that idea processors are not useful but only that, for most normal writing tasks, they're not as useful as they might appear. In making this claim, I can only talk about normal, reasonable use—using the tool as the designers intended it should be used—and even then I will probably get the Association of Backhoe Owners mad at me.

Hence, to show you how and why these programs fail, I will merely describe their basic limitations and, by presenting some simple examples, try to give you an

---

[4] I follow John Searle in rejecting these ideas about meaning. See "Literal Meaning," *Expression and Meaning* (Cambridge, England: Cambridge University Press, 1979) and "Are Meanings in the Head?" *Intentionality* (Cambridge, England: Cambridge University Press, 1983).

intuitive grasp of how these limitations affect your writing and thinking. The basic limitations are these:

1. The meaning of an item in a list (such as an outline) is not stable. The meaning depends, for example, on the other items in the list, the reason why the item appeared, the facts about the item that are known to be relevant, and the author's purpose.
2. The symbol that represents the meaning must change when any of the things the item depends on (such as the author's purpose or the other items in the list) change.

These limitations have a very simple consequence: To use idea processors effectively, you have to constantly update the lists they help you create. Because the meanings of all the items shift whenever you move items around or alter your purpose, you can't change the lists with any precision by using the program's commands alone. Whenever you use a program command, you also have to adjust three things: your idea of what the item means, your idea of what the other items mean, and the symbol that represents the item.

An example will help. I have the habit of making lists of things to do. When I first got "MaxThink," I thought I could make my life much simpler by putting together all the lists I make. Suppose I had a list of things to do this week, like the one shown in Table 9.4. I now want to compile a new list: things to do today. If I use an idea processor, the best I can easily get is something like the list shown in Table 9.5. What I want, of course is something like Table 9.6.

I admit that this is a simple-minded point and, in this form, doesn't seem too serious an objection to idea processors. I can, after all, change the entries as I move them, or if I am too lazy to do that, I can remember that, in the new list, the meaning of "buy groceries," for example, is different.

When list processing gets more complicated, however, it is not easy to do either of these things. Updating a big list is a tremendous chore. Yet failing to update the list requires that I remember the new (or old) meaning; I, at least, have a very hard time doing that. To show you how really difficult this problem is, let me give you another example, an entirely immediate one. Let us look at an outline of this paper's overall structure and compare it to an outline of this section of the paper. I gave you an outline of the overall structure at the end of the introductory section. In Table 9.7 I reproduce it. In Table 9.8 I list the things I'm discussing right now—essentially, my outline for this page and the pages surrounding it. Now try to fit the second list into the first list. As you can see, it's not at all easy. Does this mean that I'm writing badly, that I'm straying from

Table 9.4. A List Entered on "MaxThink"

Things To Do This Week

A. Work on idea processing paper
B. Buy groceries
C. Do laundry
D. Write letter to AE
E. Grade papers for technical writing class

Table 9.5. A List Constructed by Moving Entries from the Old List

Things To Do Today

A. Work on idea processing paper
B. Buy groceries
C. Grade papers for technical writing class

my outline? You can determine the answer yourself: Try to remember whether you thought I was straying before you reached this page. If you did think I was straying, perhaps I was. If you didn't, then you have grasped the structure of this, even though it's difficult for you to explain it. Most readers of this paper's drafts had no problems.

This simple example makes an important point about writing and reading processes. Most modern theorists of language comprehension believe that, when you read any comprehensible piece of prose, you first set up a master outline of the piece and then hang each idea somewhere in that outline as you read;[5] if you get lost, you haven't set the master outline up properly. If this theory is right and if my paper is comprehensible, you shouldn't have any problem combining the outlines in Tables 9.7 and 9.8, because that's what you do anyway, as you read. That the outlines don't combine easily, then, suggests that the theory is wrong. If most people have no trouble reading my paper but do have trouble constructing outlines of it, something is wrong with the cognitive thesis.

I have a noncognitive explanation of why it is so difficult to meld the two outlines. When we understand an outline, we do more than work with its symbols. We supply relationships between the items, intuit the author's purposes in making the outline, think of relevant ideas the author hasn't mentioned, employ our habits of evaluating relevance, and decide what the items in the outline mean. When we try to combine the two outlines, we have to break the glue that held together the items in each outline and try to supply new glue.[6] That glue and our intentions as readers make up the meaning that we give each item in the outline; that glue makes each item's meaning depend on its

Table 9.6. The New List with the Entries Modified Appropriately

Things To Do Today

Develop second section more fully
Buy cucumbers
Grade 3 (?) papers

---

[5] This is one way of putting the underlying thesis of cognitive psychology. The essential idea is that people process and store information by using list structures. An outline is a list structure. For a typical example, see Kintsch.

[6] There is no standard set of technical terms with which I can describe this phenomenon. In phenomenology, the items supplied which allow us to understand whatever it is we're actively aware of are in what is called a "horizon of consciousness"—the analogy is to our horizon of vision—but there is no adequate account of how we have to rearrange that horizon in order to make two quite disparate things make sense in terms of each other.

Table 9.7. **List of Things I Said I Would Discuss**

I. Look at the claims.
II. Look at the programs.
    A. Practical evaluation.
    B. Not too useful.
        1. Unless you want to put a lot of time into them.

context.[7] To manipulate the meanings and not just the symbols requires that the glue be dissolved and then reapplied. But idea processors can't dissolve and reapply the glue; they can only move symbols around.

Rearranging the items in a list can change the meaning of the items in the list because each item derives its meaning from the huge array of ideas, memories, and purposes the reader brings to it, and because these ideas, memories, and purposes depend on context. In the following example, a list of two items, I can change the meaning of each item by changing the context slightly.

Lions
Tigers

Consider what happens when I add an item.

Lions
Tigers
Wolves

This is, let us say, a list of large carnivores. Now let's replace the last item with a different one.

Lions
Tigers
Pistons

This is a list of Detroit's professional sports teams. Replace the last item again.

Lions
Tigers
Bears

Oh, my.

Even changing the title can make a huge difference. If I were to take the first list and call it "Large North American Carnivores," both the meaning of each item and the glue that holds the list together would change. The list would now suggest that all the animals inhabit the same ecosystem.

You can see now why people might have a hard time if they wanted to write papers or reports by expanding outlines. As an outline expands, the meanings of the entries, the relationships among the entries, and the appropriate symbols for the entries all change. We know this intuitively when we try to write from an outline because we find that, as we write, headings become subheadings, topics get split up

[7] In this last sentence, the glue is what John Searle, Hubert L. Dreyfus, and Ludwig Wittgenstein call "the Background." See John R. Searle, *Intentionality* (Cambridge, England: Cambridge University Press, 1983).

Table 9.8.   List of Things I'm Now Talking About

1. Anything can be useful.
2. Look at limitations.
   2.1.   Appropriate meaning is contextually determined.
   2.2.   Appropriate symbol is contextually determined.
3. Meanings are unstable.
4. Examples.
   4.1   Grocery example.
   4.2   Paper example.
   4.3   Lions–Tigers list example.

or eliminated, and ideas or facts that we thought were telling become defanged. This happens, of course, because the contexts of the entries, our purposes, and the world of relevant knowledge we bring to the outline have all changed, and this changes the entries' meanings.

The problem with idea processors, then, is that they are insensitive to changes in meaning. How serious a problem is that? Consider the list of "MaxThink" commands given in Table 9.1 and ask yourself how many of those commands you would find useful if you were working with large blocks of text or lists with many items. Surely not any of the advanced commands. Even the simple commands, the ones that make it easy to produce an outline, will interfere when you try to turn the outline into prose or when you try to update many entries.

IT'S NOT A BUG, BUT A FEATURE

There is a simple reply to these objections. If, in fact, manipulating an outline requires us to update it, and if, in fact, updating it requires us to rethink what we're doing (which groceries? Aha, cucumbers), then using an idea processor forces us to rethink. For the enthusiasts, this is not a bug but a feature, a terrific feature. Again let me quote Larson. Using "MaxThink," the promotional material says, allows you to perform "careful mental exploration of the boundaries of your . . . information" (P 3). It "lets you purposely shift your perspectives to gain as much information as possible." Using it "enables you to shift your viewpoints to bypass your current perceptions and attain additional insights."

Larson is clearly right, in a sense. Any time we rethink our meaning, new ideas may occur to us and gaps in our reasoning may appear. This is what people like Ann Berthoff are trying to get at when they claim that writing is thinking.[8] When you write, when you put down ideas in words and so objectify what you have to say, you discover new relationships among the ideas. Thus, if you believe people like Berthoff, you have to believe people like Larson, at least a little bit, because updating outlines is vaguely similar to (re)writing.

This account, unfortunately, misrepresents thinking. True, we get new ideas by writing or by updating outline entries, but we can also get new ideas by con-

---

[8] See *Forming/Thinking/Writing: The Composing Imagination*. Not that Berthoff would approve of idea processors.

templating our navels or hopping in our cars and driving around. When we evaluate this or any other claim about techniques that help us think, we must consider whether they direct our thoughts in productive ways. Writing, for example, is a productive way to make an argument or to clarify an abstract argument, because, for some reason, germane objections, relevant side issues, and felicitous ways of expressing ourselves occur to us when we write. By contrast, contemplating our navels rarely improves our thinking about an argument, and driving is often counterproductive. We can even intuitively see how writing may help us think productively and how navel contemplation may not. So the question to ask about idea processors is not whether they can help us think but whether they can help us think productively—whether updating lists is more likely to distract us (forcing useless patterns of thought on us) or whether it will bring us new insights.

Well, we've got the right question now, and I think if you're with me at all, you know what I think the answer is. But I can't prove it. The trouble is twofold. First, in any creative endeavor, you have to maintain a balance between working in a directed way toward the goal and relaxing a bit, trying to see things in a new light or getting a new idea from left field. Sometimes it's better to go for a drive. Second, in any creative endeavor, people can learn to make almost any method productive. Some people can get ideas only when they go for a drive. Similarly, idea processors could be used as a way to relax, or as a way to be directed—an inadequate way generally, but a way that practice and adaptation make adequate for some people.

I can't recommend that you learn how to use an idea processor as a tool for directed thinking, because it's obviously the wrong sort of tool. But perhaps it could be a handy tool for nondirected thinking. Perhaps a convenient outlinemaker allows us some free play of ideas. Perhaps, indeed. But it does seem to me that this doesn't happen. The most compelling reason to me is that it doesn't happen when I use the program. More compelling to you might be the reason why.

When I try to look at what I've done, searching for new ideas, holes, or a different viewpoint, I find that I have to range widely over all my material. I find, for instance, that when I review notes, it's helpful to have the notes all over the table, so that I can move quickly from one to another. If we take the notes as a metaphor for the mind, I find that the items on the fringe of my (visual, mental) horizon change the shape of the rest of what I see. One little idea, something I'm not even paying attention to, out there on the fringes of my note cards, may cause me to see my whole project differently. This is, by the way, a normal experience in other contexts; in ambiguous pictures (like Necker cubes), changing the background even slightly changes the way we see the picture. I'm arguing that our perceptions are equally changeable when we are planning a paper.

If that is the case, then any feature of a thought-supporting tool (whether an idea processor or putting note cards all over the table) that impedes our ranging freely is a bug, not a feature. For pencil-and-paper outlines, the fact that you have to mess up the page to reorder items is a bug. The fact that, when you go more than a few levels deep, your sub-sub-sub-sub-headings hit the page's right margin is another bug. Idea processors have an equivalent bug: They let you see only a few levels—usually two, a heading and its sub-headings—at a time. You can't ever range freely over the headings on the computer screen. If you're working with a four-deep outline (heading, sub-heading, sub-sub-heading, sub-sub-sub-heading), you may have quite a time even *finding* another relevant entry in a different section of the outline.

Unfortunately this is a serious bug. If any entry's meaning depends on its context, and if much of this context is invisible (not displayed on the screen), then any work you have done with one set of entries in front of you becomes obsolete as soon as almost any other entries come into view. Paper-and-pencil outlines may be clumsy because they are hard to update, but, at least while you're working with them, you can update in a relatively purposive way, because all the relevant information is visible. Moreover, paper-and-pencil outlines give you more ways to represent relationships. You can underline, draw arrows, circle items, shade, highlight, or cross out. With such techniques you can make very delicate adjustments in the context and thus range over the ideas with rather fine purposes. "Aha, this goes here" and "Oh, I might bring in a shaded reference to that over in this spot" can all be represented with an arrow, but they can't even be thought with an idea processor.

An idea processor, in other words, is likely to discourage rather than facilitate both directed and free play with ideas. True, the idea processor makes manipulation of outline entries easier, but it does this by hiding the context, and it is the context, the fringes of consciousness, that must be available if free-ranging over your ideas is to be productive. One can learn how to use idea processors for directed and free play with ideas. But there is no *a priori* reason to think that they are designed for or suited to this kind of free-ranging, no reason to think that they are precision cutting tools rather than backhoes.

SOME MORALS OF THE STORY

Can idea processors be useful? Yes, no question about it. Are they likely to be useful to the average writer? No. Are they likely to be useful to people who regularly plan with outlines, who tend to write things they are sure about, and who rarely update entries in paper-and-pencil outlines? Yes. Will idea processors make writing easier by making writing from outlines easier? No, because the usefulness of writing from outlines very much depends on having the whole outline in front of you so that you can understand each item in its context. Will idea processors help writers who write by expanding each outlined item? Yes, but unless these writers are very skilled, idea processors will only reinforce what I think is an ineffective way to plan and write. Should you use idea processors? Who knows. If you think you might, invest in "MaxThink" and find out.

I could stop here. Before I quit, however, I want to bring out some other consequences of this discussion. If my observations about the weaknesses of idea processors are at all valid, they pose two previously unnoticed problems for modern accounts of the writing process. The first problem is that the writing process in my account has at least two distinct steps. In the first, we might put down symbols for ideas and give them some kind of provisional relationship; we gather what we have to say and allocate a position in the hierarchy to each item. That stage, in the classic accounts of the writing process, is the outlining stage. In the second, we expand on those ideas, make them more precise and detailed, and put them into a more precise relationship. This relationship is not a more precise definition of order and importance (which is what the outline gave us); the second step does not hang each item on a more precisely defined branch. Rather, in the second step we give the ideas different kinds of relationships, those offered us by the endless resources of English prose. Relationships of order and importance fall by the wayside. This second stage, in the classic accounts, is the writing stage.

I'm not suggesting that we return to the classic accounts of the writing process. But I would like to point out that authoritative modern accounts, such as those given by Linda Flower and John R. Hayes (1980, 1981), do not make any distinction between the two steps. Flower and Hayes describe formal or procedural processes for solving writing problems that would apply equally well whether we were outlining or writing. Yet the simple fact that idea processors fail for a normal user (me) who wishes to write by expanding the entries in an outline suggests that the procedures need to be different. Perhaps, as my discussion suggests, the more finely grained, the more rich and detailed the context you know to be relevant (what you've written before), the thicker becomes the glue that holds items together, and the less useful it is to do formal manipulations.

The second problem facing modern accounts of the writing process is this: The first step in the writing process seems to be more free-ranging than Flower and Hayes's account suggests. Flower and Hayes (and all other cognitivists) describe writing as a problem-solving process (1981). This implies that, once a problem is solved, it's solved, so that one can (usually) work on things piecemeal. But if idea processors fail because they don't allow you to range freely in the early going—when all relationships among ideas are flexible and open to question, and when many different activities, including the contemplation of one's navel, might be helpful— then the writing process in its early stages stops looking like a problem-solving process, because it isn't closed and it doesn't move steadily toward a solution.

Idea processors do have one use: to help us study the writing process. The way idea processors interfere with people's purposes during the writing process can tell us something interesting about what the writers are trying to do. Such a study would have to recognize the vast differences in individual writing styles, and it would have to recognize that any writing process is determined by the meaning of what the author has already written. A study that takes these considerations accurately into account (no mean task) could either confirm or discredit my somewhat impressionistic, personal, and intuitive criticism of idea processors. More important, the study's results could teach us something new about a completely mysterious, endlessly fascinating subject: the writing process.

REFERENCES

Berthoff, Ann. *Forming/Thinking/Writing: The Composing Imagination.* Upper Montclair, N.J.: Boynton/Cook Publishers, 1978.

Dreyfus, H. *What Computers Can't Do,* rev. ed. New York: Harper & Row, 1979.

Flower, Linda, and John R. Hayes. "A Cognitive Process Theory of Writing." *College Composition and Communication* 32 (December 1981): 359–382.

———. "Identifying the Organization of Writing Processes." In *Cognitive Processes in Writing.* Hillsdale, N.J.: Erlbaum, 1980.

Haugeland, John. "Semantic Engines." In *Mind Design,* edited by John Haugeland. Cambridge, Mass.: M.I.T. Press, 1981.

Kintsch, Walter. *The Representation of Meaning in Memory.* Hillsdale, N.J.: Erlbaum, 1974.

Putnam, Hilary. "The Meaning of Meaning." In *Collected Papers.* Cambridge, Mass.: Harvard University Press, 1984.

Searle, John R. *Intentionality.* Cambridge, England: Cambridge University Press, 1983.

———. "Literal Meaning." In *Expression and Meaning.* Cambridge, England: Cambridge University Press, 1979.

Expert Systems, Artificial Intelligence, and the Teaching of Writing

JOHN E. THIESMEYER

Despite the emergence of a number of computer-based aids for the writer and writing teacher—"prewriters" to develop strategies; "idea processors" to generate outlines; checkers for spelling, mechanics and usage; statistical text analyzers, and so on—developers of writing programs do not lack challenges. Even if we assume that present aids are effective (and those returns are not yet in), a number of writing problems remain that we cannot process artificially except under severe constraints. These range from sentence fragments, comma splices, and malformed sentences to more comprehensive issues of coherence, argument, tone, and style.

Recently, the software industry has begun a sales campaign for sophisticated programs, described as "artificially intelligent," that are claimed to imitate human analytic and problem-solving activities. "Superbrains . . . the new generation of 'intelligent' software," trumpets an advertisement for a book on expert systems: "programs so smart, they actually employ the same reasoning processes as human experts" (*InfoWorld* 25 March 1985, 54).

The question I propose to consider is whether artificial-intelligence (AI) programming can address the larger problems in composition instruction that I have mentioned. How effective will computers ultimately become in diagnosing and remedying poor writing and in promoting good writing?

For purposes of this discussion we can use the working definition of AI offered in a standard text, the *Handbook of Artificial Intelligence*: A computer system is "intelligent" if it "exhibit[s] the characteristics we associate with intelligence in human behavior—understanding language, learning, reasoning, solving problems, and so on" (Barr, 3). The definition is typical of the field. It is circular, behavioral, and pragmatic, incorporating the famous test proposed by early computer scientist Alan Turing: If we cannot tell the difference between a machine's behavior and a human's, the machine must be presumed intelligent. The problem of what constitutes intelligence in itself is thus set aside, and much artificial-intelligence research has followed a precept that might be worded "Investigate what human beings do, in various situations, and program computers to do it as well—or better."

In these terms, say the authors of the *Handbook*, "AI researchers have invented dozens of programming techniques that support some sort of intelligent behavior," and they add, "there is every evidence that these developments will lead to a new, *intelligent technology* that may have dramatic effects on our society" (Barr, 3).

Despite the claims of advertisers and the optimism of most AI researchers, I will argue that the prospect of full partnership with intelligent machines in composition teaching is not immediate—and is probably not even distant. That conclusion arises from a variety of considerations, including the state of our linguistic understanding, the beliefs underlying most artificial-intelligence research, a computational phenomenon known as "combinatorial explosion," and some discoveries based on practical experience with computer-aided instruction in writing.

Let me take the last first. Over the past two years, I have worked with several hundred college students using text-analysis programs in conjunction with microcomputer word processors as aids in the learning of writing. I have used these aids in a variety of academic contexts: in expository composition courses with both freshmen and upperclass students, in required freshman general-education courses, and with seniors and juniors writing honors papers and required interdisciplinary essays.

A predictable discovery seems crucial to the present question: Students have a low tolerance for errors in pedagogic software. For instance, in our writing lab we use a spelling checker (Radio Shack's "Scripsit Dictionary") that has a stored lexicon of about 73,000 words. It is well suited to a teaching environment because it does not offer mindlessly to "correct" typos and misspellings it finds, as other checkers do, but simply flags the problem and invites the student to do something about it— usually by consulting a dictionary.

Most students are at first delighted with this assistance, but their behavior changes after they find, as they inevitably do, that the checker sometimes flags perfectly ordinary words as possible misspellings. However far it may exceed any individual's command of the language, 73,000 words inadequately represents the working vocabulary of a *group* of typical college students (Thiesmeyer, 1985, 280–281). As soon as they realize the program is fallible, many students return to their own shaky orthographic intuitions. Instead of looking up a spelling the program questions, if it "looks all right" to them they will often assume the software has stumbled again and leave the word unchanged.

For usage and mechanics we use a software system descended, like several sold commercially, from part of Bell Labs' "Writer's Workbench." We think our version is the best around, because it has been carefully developed and tested by real English teachers and presently incorporates a dictionary of over 3000 common errors in usage and mechanics made by inexperienced writers (Thiesmeyer, 1984). The system, which we call "Editor," identifies a high proportion of clumsy locutions in student papers. But, by the very nature of such programs, which rely on "string" or "pattern" matching independent of semantic content, it can often only query a word or phrase and ask for judgment. When it flags *chairman* as gender-specific, for example, "Editor" does not know whether the text's referent is explicitly male and the term appropriate; when it says of *effect*, "commonly misused word: do you mean *affect*?" only the writer can respond.

Here again, student skepticism soon surfaces. After finding in several instances that the original wording was correct, a student often generalizes to other cases and begins ignoring many of the program's editorial promptings. Thus one who uses *effect* and *affect* correctly may rashly assume that he or she has a similar facility with *choose* and *chose*, *their* and *there*, or *imply* and *infer*. I have had a difficult time convincing students that, when the program notes a particular usage, it means that there is a reasonable chance that the usage is wrong and should be reconsidered.

This behavior is the reverse of—and sometimes a reaction to—the initial impulse of some students to treat any message from a checker program as gospel, which leads them, in turn, to make ill-considered and unnecessary changes. That is a different problem—and an easier one to deal with because students more readily accept an instruction to start exercising their own judgment (rather than relying on the computer) than they are to stop.

Students' mistrust of software on the basis of its presumed fallibility could have been predicted. After all, they treat us human pedagogical devices no differently. But students accept a teacher's fallibility more readily than a computerized text analyzer's; when students use the software, they tolerate very little ambiguity or error, no matter how sound the software's theoretical foundations (see Daiute, 127).

That conclusion brings us to the question of how effectively we can design programs to eliminate such perceived weaknesses. Using AI programming techniques, can we hope to simulate the editorial accuracy of, say, an ordinary English teacher with a couple of decades of experience?

Consider for a moment the common claim that "expert systems" are a successful example of artificial-intelligence programming. An expert system is a type of computer program that stores some of the information human experts have about a particular well-defined area of interest and applies the information in answering questions or solving problems within that area. Noted expert systems are currently helping diagnose infectious diseases, identify chemical and geological formations, and configure computer installations. Despite their sometimes complex structures and the aura of mystery and glamor that publicists endow them with, expert systems are conceptually rather simple. Their essential components are the "decision" or "production" rules that specify how each program will respond to the information it is given. These rules often take the form of straightforward "if–then" instructions: If X is the case, then do Y.

Note that expert systems do not themselves make crucial decisions. Those have already been made by the experts consulted and have been programmed into the decision rules. The systems can only apply the rules, albeit more rapidly, more comprehensibly—and less flexibly—than their human mentors. (See Cendrowska and Bramer for a detailed study of a prominent expert system.)

It follows that, no matter how sophisticated its design or how ingenious its programming, the worth of an expert system in any practical context is directly proportional to the quality of its "knowledge base": the information about real-world states of affairs supplied by human beings. An expert system is only a device for the systematic application of already-existing knowledge. Without knowledge that is comprehensive, clearly represented in terms accessible to the program, and (above all) accurate within its proper domain, such a system will fail of its purpose.

What is true of expert systems, designed for use only in restricted contexts, applies more broadly to AI systems aiming to represent more general kinds of human behavior, including language use. Whether artificial-intelligence programming can help us teach writing depends heavily on our ability to represent, in programming terms, the subtle structures and contents of the language we teach—especially when we take into account the limitations of expert systems and student mistrust of fallible software. Representing language programmatically, in turn, depends on how well we understand our language, not as native speakers exercising our inherent competencies but as objective analysts and system builders. If we cannot satisfactorily represent natural human languages as formal systems—as finite sets of symbols and rules—the way we represent mathematical and other artificial languages, we cannot develop fully competent expert systems for language instruction. At some level, of course, most of us *believe* languages are formal systems, if we believe they are produced by brains and are therefore subject to the ultimate determinism of physical law. But complete physical descriptions of brain functions are a long way off, and it remains for us to discover in the interim whether we can fully understand natural languages by other means.

A great deal of work has been going forward in the artificial simulation of human language processing. Remarkable results are being achieved in this direction, and more are promised. Many readers will have heard that, in text analysis, "Writer's Workbench" and IBM's "Epistle" can already go beyond mere spelling, mechanics, and usage checking to the discovery of some syntactic errors in texts; and the pedagogical millennium may appear close at hand (see Miller, Heidorn, and Jensen for a typical description and discussion).

A review of the past three decades of linguistic research should give us pause, however. The brilliant promise of the transformational-generative syntactic models developed by Noam Chomsky and others—models of such clarity and high formalism that full-scale machine translation among natural languages was for some years confidently anticipated—has given way to disillusioning debates over whether syntax can be considered central to language understanding at all. Similarly, generative semantics and other meaning-centered grammars, though correcting the anti-semantic bias of early transformationalism, have failed fully to analyze natural language. The problems of contemporary linguistics are deep and severe enough to offer scant hope for an early solution.

An analogous debate is under way in the artificial-intelligence and natural-language-processing communities today. On the one hand are builders of elaborate phrase-structure models of syntax, of the sort inspired by Chomsky and partly embodied in many syntax-analysis programs. On the other are self-styled "cognitive scientists" attempting to represent human semantic intuitions formally, but with little hope of reconciling competing theories any time soon.

Optimistic expectations for computerized natural-language analysis are excessive, considering what we currently know we don't know about language. They are partly motivated by the plausibility and ingenuity of what even a limited programmed model of some of a language's features can accomplish. I would offer several observations about such provisional models. Though computers can model "context-free" languages (Cook, 406), research has not demonstrated, even theoretically, that they can model "context-determined" languages like English. As Chomsky has noted, each advance in our linguistic knowledge has shown that "what can be seen to lie beyond the scope of present understanding and technique [is] far more remote than was heretofore imagined" (Chomsky, 5). There is a difference between *imitation* of language behavior, which computers can be made rather good at, and computer *analysis* of a natural language similar to that practiced by writing teachers. Imitation requires only a limited set of rules; analysis requires an understanding of the language, and maybe even an awareness of human experience. The fact that a computer can now tell us, in nearly natural tones, how much money to deposit for a long-distance call holds no promise for solving the analytic problems. (Perhaps the most lucid survey and discussion of the theoretical issues in natural-language processing is Winograd's.)

Not only do natural languages (and their most ambitious computer simulations) require a stored lexicon of morphemes or word elements and a set of rules for arranging them, but they also require that the items in the lexicon be *labeled* ("marked," in linguistic terms) for their attributes and functions within the language (Pearson, 187–230). Thus, in analyzing syntactic structures, programs like "Writer's Workbench" and "Epistle" make use of large stored vocabularies of words labeled with their grammatical functions. The programs can thereby identify the roles of most words in a text and, by comparing their arrangements with the stored rules of correct syntax, can identify many ill-formed sentences. I have been told that "Workbench" has a stored lexicon of about 100,000 words, and IBM has for many years been developing a similar file. Labeled lists of such size may well approximate the working vocabularies of such human groups as college students, though such lists cannot by themselves resolve the semantic ambiguities that often forestall purely syntactic analysis.

Moreover, to my knowledge, such analyses can be carried out today only on large computers, because of the sheer numbers of comparisons required to analyze even a simple text syntactically. Speed and storage problems will certainly diminish, of course, and tomorrow's micros will exceed today's mainframes in computing strength. There remains a computability problem, however, because the mere size of a working vocabulary does not determine how much computing power may be needed to analyze its parent language. That measure depends, instead, on the number of possible relationships among words and rules that the computer must examine.

Let me clarify this point by analogy. Roughly speaking, a rule of sentence structure stored in a program can be thought of as containing a number of abstract "slots"—representations of parts of speech or of meanings—that could in practice be filled by vocabulary words, each capable of having several meanings. An analytic procedure must identify the words in an actual sentence, work out all the possible combinations (the ambiguities) of function and meaning among the words, and check the results against the list of rules until it finds a match. Each sentence can thus invoke a number of combinations to be checked. Though a computer analysis would not be so inefficient as my analogy makes it sound, the principle holds that, for complex rules and large vocabularies, the numbers of combinations to be checked can become very large indeed.

We do not know at present how many rules will suffice to describe the sentences of a natural language; we know only that the number must be large. The task is not just to discover the fundamental rules of sentence organization but also to enumerate the myriad exceptions—for, of course, exceptions are also rules. At every turn the investigator finds extraordinarily complex interactions between syntax and semantics, between texts and contexts, driving the number of rules up. This complexity causes a computability problem: As the number of interrelationships to be examined rises, the number of computations needed rises factorially. A "combinatorial explosion" occurs, and the computations rapidly become too numerous for even the largest machines to handle.

The scope of such combinatorial explosions can be illustrated by the simple computer card—remember those? The number of possible patterns of holes in an ordinary computer punch-card is 2 to the 960th power, a number larger than the cube of the estimated number of particles in the universe (Andrew, 26). If a natural language turns out to allow as many possible patterns as even such a small card may hold, no linear computer of any attainable power will be able to carry out full-scale linguistic analyses of the sort an English teacher performs every week. Although leaders of the Japanese "Fifth-Generation Project" hope by the mid-1990s to create super-micros 30,000 times more powerful than today's, even with such machines they expect the natural-language operating system to have no more than a 10,000-word vocabulary and 2000 syntactic rules (Shapiro, 640).

Research into the problems and prospects of natural-language processing by computer will no doubt continue to have provocative implications for linguistics and psychology. In the words of a standard textbook in computation theory, however, "from a formal standpoint" the task of producing a fully realized English language analyzer "may be impossible" (Lewis and Papadimitriou, 95–96). One of the recognized pioneers in the study of natural-language processing by computer, Terry Winograd, now thinks "the idea . . . that language and thought can be modeled by such things as formal logic . . . is grossly oversimplified" (quoted in Waldrop, 44). So the best analytic programs we can hope for may be fundamentally limited—if not in vocabulary then in scope, in what might be called "understanding" of syntax and meaning. As I have suggested, syntactic and semantic text analysis using less-than-competent linguistic models, even those produced for the advanced machines of the next decade, may offer limited help in teaching composition to typical undergraduates.

Though limited, the assistance may nevertheless be welcome. It is no small thing, after all, that a computer program can identify over 10,000 locutions characteristic of poor writing (that is the present compass of our "Editor" text analyzer, using "wild-card" searches to include variant forms), enabling the student to improve his or her usage, often substantially, before submitting the paper for evaluation.

A few more comments about artificial intelligence and its long-term prospects will conclude these remarks. From its beginnings in the work of people like Herbert Simon, contemporary with the beginnings of transformational-generative linguistic theory in the 1950s, artificial-intelligence research has been haunted by an *a priori* notion of what intelligence is. The researchers have assumed that computers can employ the same reasoning processes as human beings—a belief that further assumes that we know what human reasoning is and that reasoning is a strictly logical, rule-governed process at higher than neurological levels in the mind. Simon believes (as do most builders of expert systems) that human intelligence can be largely equated with problem-solving procedures and that these procedures can be made explicit by simple introspection or query techniques (see Simon, 14 ff.; Feigenbaum and McCorduck, II–III).

Such beliefs have been acutely described by modern historians of science: They are "paradigmatic," to use Thomas Kuhn's well-known term, or "thematic," to use Gerald Holton's—"the (usually unacknowledged) presuppositions pervading the work of scientists" over long periods (Holton, 29). These paradigms or themes tend to be unexamined by those holding them. They have the force of axioms, and of course they radically condition understanding.

The theme of formal intelligibility, as I would call it, is as old as Plato's cognitive line, and it appears to dominate much of today's thinking about artificial intelligence. But this presupposition is drastically limiting; "programs that draw exclusively on logic are capturing only part of the understanding of an intelligent person" (Lenat, 207). The assumption of formal intelligibility ignores the possibility that the experiences we call by names like "insight" and "intuition" are valid components of thinking, even of reasoning (Waldrop). Because those components are part of the vast "hidden" structures of the unconscious mind and are therefore not open to logical inspection, Hubert Dreyfus and others have strongly challenged the idea that a satisfactory formal model of thinking can ever be devised.

Thus the question of whether computers can process natural language mirrors larger questions of mind and brain, of artificial and natural intelligence. We cannot devise algorithms to represent those parts of either writing or thinking that we do not understand, and insofar as much of what happens in our minds is hidden, we may never fully understand these processes. One might object that, as a physical object, the *brain* is not hidden, but even a full physical description of the brain would not necessarily lead to a computable model of thought. A. K. Dewdney has pointed out, following the work of physicist Stephen Wolfram at Princeton, that some natural systems that store, transmit, and manipulate information may consist of "rather simple components whose combined behavior is so complex that it may not be reducible to a mathematical statement—its best description is itself" (Dewdney, 18, 30; see also Wolfram, 198–203). I have encountered no speculations about brains in this regard, but a brain's components are not simple. I conjecture that the human brain comprises just such a natural system, computationally irreducible—that even in its role as a language-analyzing device, it cannot be modeled algorithmically. If so, the only competent model of its functions would be itself or another human brain.

We may conclude, then, that teachers and students of writing must remain indefinitely dependent. Their dependency will rest not on machines or programs, however, but principally where it has lain all along: on their own marvelous and mysterious linguistic abilities. Programmed intelligences, unable to approximate those abilities, will play a supporting role at best. This conclusion may or may not be comforting.

REFERENCES

Andrew, A. M. *Artificial Intelligence*. Tunbridge Wells, Kent, England: Abacus, 1983.

Barr, Avron, and Edward A. Feigenbaum, eds. *Handbook of Artificial Intelligence*. Vol. 1. Los Altos, Calif.: William Kaufmann, 1981.

Cendrowska, Jadzia, and Max Bramer. "Inside an Expert System: A Rational Reconstruction of the MYCIN Consultation System." In *Artificial Intelligence: Tools, Techniques, and Applications*, edited by Tim O'Shea and Marc Eisenstadt. New York: Harper & Row, 1984.

Chomsky, Noam. *Language and Mind*, enlarged ed. New York: Harcourt, 1972.

Cook, Stephen A. "An Overview of Computational Complexity." Turing Award Lecture. *Communications of the ACM* 26 (1983): 400–408.

Daiute, Colette. *Writing and Computers*. Reading, Mass.: Addison-Wesley, 1985.

Dewdney, A. K. "Computer Recreations." *Scientific American*, May 1985: 18–30.

Dreyfus, Hubert L. *What Computers Can't Do: The Limits of Artificial Intelligence*. Revised ed. New York: Harper & Row, 1979.

———. "A Framework for Misrepresenting Knowledge." In *Philosophical Perspectives in Artificial Intelligence*, edited by Martin Ringle. Atlantic Highlands, N.J.: Humanities, 1979, pp. 124–136.

Feigenbaum, Edward A., and Pamela McCorduck. *The Fifth Generation: Artificial Intelligence and Japan's Computer Challenge to the World*. New York: NAL, 1984.

Holton, Gerald. *Thematic Origins of Scientific Thought: Kepler to Einstein*. Cambridge, Mass.: Harvard University Press, 1973.

Lenat, Douglas. "Computer Software for Intelligent Systems." *Scientific American*. September 1984: 204–213.

Lewis, Harry R., and Christos H. Papadimitriou. *Elements of the Theory of Computation*. Englewood Cliffs, N.J.: Prentice-Hall, 1981.

Miller, Lance A., George E. Heidorn, and Karen Jensen. "Text-Critiquing with the EPISTLE System: An Author's Aid to Better Syntax." *AFIPS Conference Proceedings: 1981 National Computer Conference*. 50. Arlington: AFIPS Press, 1981, pp. 649–655.

Pearson, Bruce L. *Introduction to Linguistic Concepts*. New York: Knopf, 1977.

Shapiro, Ehud Y. "The Fifth Generation Project—A Trip Report." *Communications of the ACM* 26 (1983): 637–641.

Simon, Herbert. "Is Thinking Uniquely Human?" *University of Chicago Magazine*. Fall 1981: 12–21.

Thiesmeyer, John. "Some Boundary Considerations for Writing-Software." In *Computers and Composition: Selected Papers from the Conference on Computers and Writing*, edited by Lillian Bridwell and Donald Ross. NP: Colorado State and Michigan Technological University, 1985.

———. "Teaching with the Text Checkers." In *The Written Word and the Word Processor*, edited by Thomas E. Martinez. Villanova, Penna.: Villanova University, 1984, pp. 280–290.

Waldrop, M. Mitchell. "Machinations of Thought." *Science 85* March 1985: 38–45.

Winograd, Terry. "Computer Software for Working with Language." *Scientific American*. September 1984: 131–145.

Wolfram, Stephen. "Computer Software in Science and Mathematics." *Scientific American*. September 1984: 188–203.

In Search of the Writon

MICHAEL E. COHEN

Before we, as writing teachers and instructional software developers, can figure out how to evaluate computers in the writing classroom, we have to establish, as precisely as we can, just what it is we are evaluating. Taking that seemingly obvious first step, however, is not so easy as it sounds. The people who give us computers (granting agencies or school administrations) want an answer, in objective and quantifiable terms, to this question: "Has the money we've spent on all of this hardware, software, and logistical support improved the quality of the writing instruction in a cost-effective way?" Often the people who ask this question expect an answer something like this: "Student writing done with computer support has improved XX percent, compared to YY percent for student writing done the traditional way." They want numerical evidence that computers have improved student writing more quickly and efficiently than noncomputerized instruction. Whether we get to keep the instructional computers we have, and whether we get to acquire more, often depends on our meeting this expectation. But what is "better" and how do you measure it? That's the problem.

Those who ask for evidence of writing improvement are not villains. They are not asking for it just to persecute writing teachers and writing-lab directors. They ask because they have responsibilities of their own that they must fulfill. Schools, granting agencies, and governments have only so much money to disburse, and they regularly receive requests for more money than they have to give. The computers and computer labs that we want are expensive propositions: To serve 500 writing students, giving each student a mere 4 hours of computer access a week, requires at least 40 computers in a lab open 50 hours each week—and this assumes that each computer is in constant use for each of those 50 hours and that no machine ever breaks down.[1] If each computer costs $2000, the lab will cost $80,000 just for the computers. Add the cost of peripheral equipment (such as printers), supplies (paper, disks, ribbons), software, furniture, security, insurance, maintenance, and—most important—qualified staff to run the operation, and we arrive at a first-year budget well in excess of $120,000. And, though lab budgets for subsequent years will be smaller than the first-year figure, they won't evaporate. So when we ask for a computer-based writing lab, we're asking someone to give us a large amount of money at once, and we're asking for a substantial amount of money for

---

[1] In practice, about half again as many machines will be needed to keep a computer-based writing lab running smoothly. The UCLA Writing Programs' computer lab has 20 computers and is open 55 hours a week. This is barely enough to serve 120 first-year composition students, or 6 classes—out of more than 50 first-year composition classes offered each quarter. In fact, to serve the 500 students in the example given, more than 40 computers would be needed, because machines *do* break down and students don't come into the lab in a steady, measured stream.

each year that the lab will be in service. Those who give us the money have not only a right, but a *responsibility*, to ask us to prove that we have spent the money wisely.

So, again, what is "better" and how do we measure it? Implicit in the question—or, rather, in the expected answer—is a description of "better" that is expressed numerically. And *this* implies, conceptually, at least, some sort of measurement unit, like "watt" or "pound." It implies a unit of measurement that I will call the *writon*, attached to a discrete number that sums up how much "better" one piece of writing is than another. This seems only natural: Dollars are expressed numerically; therefore, proof of a computer-based writing lab's cost-effectiveness should be expressed numerically. It is a logical assumption to make. It establishes a clear relationship between dollars spent and value gained. It is simple. It is tidy. It is reassuring and satisfying. Numbers that express value gained (or lost) are the natural language of budget administrators.

We need to measure writons, therefore, to demonstrate writing improvement mathematically. Even if we measure only the final written product, we can quantify many things. We can count words per essay. We can compare the number of words in a final draft to the total time the assignment took to write. We can count T-units.[2] We can measure spelling mistakes against word counts and grammar mistakes against sentence counts. We can read essays holistically and average the scores for three readings. We can score holistically for certain abstract qualities: stylistic, organizational, and creative. And on and on. The number of things we can quantify just from the final written product is very large.

No one of these measurements, however, fully describes writing improvement; no one of these is *the* unit of measurement—the writon. So that leaves us with the problem of building a statistical model to describe how all the measurements that we *can* make combine to express the writon. We need a model along the lines of this equation:

Writon = [(T-unit) × (Word/misspelling ratio)] + [(Stylistic ability) × (Organizational ability)] . . .

In other words, we need a model into which we feed certain measurements so that we can say something like "The papers written with the computer improved 14 writons more than traditionally written papers."

Let's explore the concept of a statistical model a little more deeply by drawing an analogy to a real-life model. The ARPI—the Arson Risk Prediction Index—is a tool used by the New York City Arson Strike Force to predict which buildings have the highest arson risk. The ARPI enables the Strike Force to take preventive action.[3] The ARPI is created by a rather arduous process. A number of facts about individual buildings that have experienced arson, as well as those that haven't, are collected: prior fire histories, the number of quarters each has been in tax arrears, vacancy rates, sizes, types (such as commercial or residential), locations, and so forth. These facts are fed into a statistical procedure known as *discriminant analysis*, which analyzes the facts in each category to determine which facts, or combinations of

---

[2] T-unit stands for "minimum terminable unit"—a main clause with its subordinate clauses, if any.

[3] See Bruce Dillenbeck, "Fighting Fire with Technology," *Byte* 10 (10) (October 1985): 249–251.

facts, best typify a building that has experienced arson. The result is a mathematical formula. Plug the facts about any building into the formula, and it will tell you how likely that building is to have an arson fire. The facts are called *predictor variables* because they vary from building to building and because they predict a possible occurrence. They are called *weighted* predictor variables because some are more important than others (though all have some significance). For example, a building's prior history of arson may weigh more heavily than how many vacant apartments or offices it contains.

Sounds rather straightforward, doesn't it? We could do something similar with the writon. We could collect a number of facts about good and bad student essays, feed them into a computer program that does discriminant analysis, and discover the statistical model—the relationship between all of the collected facts—that defines the writon.

But precise measurement isn't easy. Let's look more closely at the ARPI to see one reason why. In New York's Crown Heights section the year after the ARPI was established, only 13 out of 39 arsons occurred in the top 100 buildings in the ARPI high-risk list.[4] The ARPI predicted fire risk, but only weakly. What went wrong? Well, the ARPI is a model based on *city-wide* arson and building information. Crown Heights is just one section of a large, hardly uniform city. It takes a different model, one specific to the neighborhood, to give significantly better results,[5] and even then the results aren't perfect.

By analogy, a statistical model of the writon will have similar limitations. Just as an arson-risk model set up for a whole city is less accurate than one set up for a specific neighborhood, a writon model set up for all student writing will be less accurate in describing writing quality than different models set up for specific types and levels of student writing. Thus we would need specific models for first-year liberal arts students, second-year pre-law students, and so on. And we would need specific models for descriptive essays, lab reports, and all the other categories (neighborhoods) of student writing. So now we no longer have one writon but a whole family of them; our tidy unit of measurement is getting messy.

Perhaps we could live with this complicated state of affairs. Unfortunately, the ARPI and the writon only *seem* to be similar cases. Arson is what statisticians call a "bipolar phenomenon": Either there has been arson or there hasn't. Writing quality, by comparison, is not bipolar; there isn't just good writing on the one hand and bad writing on the other with nothing in between. Writing quality covers a range and depends as much on context as it does on any absolute concept of good and bad writing (a good history essay is not good for all the same reasons that make a biology lab report good). Unfortunately, discriminant analysis produces a formula only for cases in which there are just two groups,[6] so a discriminant analysis of our measurements won't give us the writon. And even if it could, the model would be tautological—to produce a statistical model that defines writing quality, we first must define . . . writing quality. The tautology arises from this statement: "We

---

[4] See Royer Cook, "Predicting Arson," *Byte* 10 (10) (October 1985): 239–245.

[5] Cook, p. 244.

[6] Dillenbeck, p. 249.

could collect a number of facts about good and bad student essays . . . ." Doing this presupposes that we already know how to define good and bad writing—that we already know, in some sense, how to define the writon. Arson is an *observable* fact. Writing quality, on the other hand, is not an observed fact but a *perceived* phenomenon.

For our model, then, we must turn to methods by which perceived qualities are evaluated. Take a set of student placement essays, like those written for UCLA's Writing Placement exam.[7] The tests are used to place students in one of three levels of first-year composition. Writing instructors, those who teach the first-year writing courses, score the tests holistically. That is, an instructor reads a test once and gives it a score based on the instructor's general impression of the test's writing quality and content. Before the scoring begins, however, the scorers must be "normed." That is, the instructors read a guide to scoring that presents a definition of writing proficiency (within the context of the exam) and then evaluate a small set of prescored essays that range from good to bad as defined by the scoring guide. The readers do this so that they can more or less align their individual judgments—their *perceptions* of writing quality—for the purposes of grading. This alignment, moreover, is not with an abstract concept of quality but with the perceptions of the person who selected the normative essays in the first place and with the perceptions of fellow scorers. Furthermore, the norming process occurs each day that tests are being scored, because even experienced readers get out of perceptual alignment with each other rather quickly. Each test is read by at least two readers, and those tests that receive significantly divergent scores are read and scored by additional readers until a consensus is reached. The whole process is not infallible, though it is reasonably fair to the students.

Note that this process does nothing more than establish a community of perception for a very specific purpose (student placement in first-year composition) and that it does so for only a short period of time. It does not and *cannot* define the writon, except for a specific group of essays on a specific topic. Even then the result is a subjective definition, yet it is as close as the University of California has come to a definition of writing quality after almost a century of the Subject A requirement.

If we define the writon in such a manner, we can't measure it in any pieces of writing except for those done in a specific setting on a specific topic. It not only reduces the writon's usefulness; it also tempts us to skew our teaching to deal with only those sorts of writing that the writon can measure.

It would be nice if the people who want us to measure writons would tell us what a writon is. But they won't. They don't really know what it is. They only know that they want it.

This means that any report that evaluates computer use in writing classrooms also has to define the writon itself. (Naturally, the writon won't be called a writon;

---

[7] Formerly known as the "Subject A" exam. Subject A is a California statute that requires students entering the University of California system to meet certain minimal standards of writing proficiency. The statute, which dates back to the nineteenth century, does not specify clearly just what those standards are.

it probably won't even be expressed as a unit of measurement. But it will be some sort of statement that defines how the study statistically represents writing quality; it will serve *functionally* as a writon.) And, in addition to providing the definition, the report will have to defend it. Furthermore, it can defend it only by proving that it really does express writing quality. And the only way that a report can prove *that* beyond doubt is by showing *how* the definition is accurate—by quantifying it. This sort of validation, in turn, can be done *formally* only by expressing that accuracy in terms of another new unit of measurement, a unit that measures the model's accuracy. For models like the ARPI, this unit is a statistical measurement known by statisticians as the "r^2"; for the writon it would be something as provisional as the writon itself: a meta-writon, if you will. It is an infinite regress. And it is an infinite regress because we are trying to objectify an aesthetic (and hence subjective) judgment.

This is, of course, something of a *reductio ad absurdum*: Most of those who want writons measured don't demand that we formally establish the writon's validity. They merely want us to persuade them that the definition is reasonable. So that leaves us, in practice, a lot of freedom in which to perform our evaluation. Our definition of the writon will depend on the expectations and knowledge of those whom we are trying to convince. If we write an evaluation for a professional journal, we will define the writon for the journal's audience. If we write one for the dean, we will define the writon for *that* audience. In essence, then, the evaluation of computer-aided writing instruction becomes a rhetorical task as much as a formal, scientific one.

But appearing to be precise and objective, when we know that this appearance disguises a fundamental subjectivity, is ultimately an intellectually dishonest task. It can't be otherwise, because, as we've seen, the writon can't be validated. It might serve our purposes and get us the machines and money that we want, but it will do little for our self-respect.

As I see it, our only way out of this thicket lies in not walking into it in the first place. We can avoid dishonesty by placing ourselves in the position of deciding what it is *we* are going to evaluate, not letting someone else decide for us. If we let someone else do it, we'll only end up having to define the writon.

The problem is one of expectations. Our benefactors expect us to provide them with results, bad or good (preferably good). In any request we make for money or machines, then, *we* must establish the form of the results that we hope to provide. All too often we request resources "to improve the quality of instruction" without ever specifying the ways in which we expect instruction to improve. Often, if not usually, we don't know ourselves. But we do have some guesses. Those whom we ask for money are not usually writing specialists, and they will not know that it is impossible to evaluate something as vague as writing quality, so they will expect results in terms of writing quality—in terms of the writon—unless, from the very beginning, we tell them otherwise. We must tell our benefactors as clearly as possible just exactly what those things are that we *can* evaluate and which of those we intend to evaluate.

And what we *should* evaluate are specific, evaluable things. We should pick some of our curricular goals and find out how well computer-assisted instruction helps us meet them. After all, we put computers in our classrooms to enhance our teaching, not replace it, and that assistance involves helping us achieve some of our teaching goals. The only really proper way to evaluate computers in the classroom is to determine whether they help us achieve *just those things* for which we acquired them. If we use computers to teach the writing process, we can measure how well CAI helps students learn the elements of that process. If we use computers to teach grammar, we can measure how well computers help students avoid grammatical errors. If we use computers to teach sentence combining, we can measure how well computers teach that. Whatever it is that we measure, we have to avoid being put in the position of proving that "writing has been made better because of computers" and instead evaluate how well computers have helped us meet the specific curricular goals for which we obtained them.

Doing this keeps us honest and, what's more, keeps us responsible. It helps us clarify for ourselves the reasons why we want the computers in the first place. It helps us clarify for ourselves what we intend to do with the computers. And it helps us acquire the knowledge we need to teach more effectively with computers.

Doing this will also satisfy our benefactors and colleagues, at least for a while. And it will prevent our being challenged to prove that writing has been made better in order to keep our instructional computers. It still begs the question, of course, because ultimately someone will still want to know whether "writing has been made better." But it will be a question asked of the whole curriculum; it won't be one that holds our computers hostage.

The Politics of CAI and Word Processing

Some Issues for Faculty and Administrators

DEBORAH H. HOLDSTEIN

Where are we now with computers and writing? It's not news to report that the practical problems of finding, implementing, and developing CAI or word processing packages can still frustrate and hinder the efforts of capable, inventive faculty. However, many colleagues across the writing curriculum who have rushed to participate in this quickly changing discipline now face issues for which they are unprepared: the political repercussions of technological interests within English and humanities departments.

In the humanities, the decision to include computers in the curriculum has added a new dimension to the traditional, if unfortunate, political battle between writing specialists and literary specialists. Within writing programs, battles erupt between pro-computer and anti-computer faculty members. And even among the pro-computer faculty, conflicts arise between those who prefer one type of software and those who champion another. Furthermore, persevering, enthusiastic instructors within the humanities often confront the condescending attitudes of programmers and technology administrators outside these departments. My failure to name names or universities in this discussion might well seem negligent; after all, it is customary to provide substantive documentation. In this instance, however, I'll risk reader skepticism in airing issues about which only a few dare speak. When it's "safe," perhaps long after this essay has appeared, my sources (and others like them) can speak forthrightly, with no risk to their tenure, their budgets, or their authority.

Consider a young professor who told me his story at a recent conference. He's one of a rare group, successfully developing computer-assisted instructional packages, working on a major project, and also marketing the CAI packages to publishers. He's been willing to tackle the creative and practical responsibilities of setting up and directing a computer-equipped writing lab as well. His department encourages his work and even seems to welcome it. Influential colleagues outside the department realize that his work enhances the university's reputation and attracts students. The Writing Technology Center, my colleague told me, is a frequent stop on tours for prospective students and is the highlight of the Board of Trustees' annual show-and-tell visit to the campus.

At tenure time? This assistant professor in an English department has been scrupulous in collecting tenure letters, wisely finding those referees who can legitimately testify that, yes, developing good software can be akin to scholarship in its most traditional sense, and who can legitimately contend that the publication contracts themselves testify to the software's significance. But colleagues in more traditional disciplines denounce the work. Perhaps they're merely unfamiliar with software development. Perhaps they're threatened by new technology. Perhaps they're genuinely concerned that technological pursuits violate the purer purposes of an English or humanities department. Whatever the reasons, by traditional standards, software compares rather badly with another tenure hopeful's book on prosody or another's on deconstruction, no matter how theory-based the software, no matter how many years of concentrated effort it demanded. Presumably, the prejudice stems from an unfortunate though familiar source, misdirected in this case: the age-old division between theory and practice. To the untrained eye, software *seems* too pedagogy-specific, relevant only to a remediation center at the university's lowest level.

Ironically, this colleague's computer-and-writing efforts have brought his university rather nice publicity; yet come tenure time, he is trapped in a debilitating double bind. Whereas the obvious signals read, "Tenure will be given for this work," the more subtle signals require more scholarly semantic decoding: "This may be good for us, and we'll be eternally grateful, but it won't necessarily be good for you." Obviously, the best research and teaching faculty in the humanities have to abandon potentially ground-breaking, computer-related work unless they can reap rewards of promotion and tenure, even though the university basks in the light of increased admissions and the favorable publicity that results from such efforts.

The irony can become even more dramatic when we consider this question: Who owns the software that faculty members develop? Universities don't claim ownership of a faculty member's book about Milton, in spite of the money the institution has indirectly contributed through secretarial help, typewriter ribbons, photocopying, and perhaps even word-processing software, disks, and computer time. The college might be able to claim that part of the author's salary paid for the time spent on the book. But, fortunately for the ways in which most faculty produce their scholarly efforts, colleges aren't suddenly interested in seizing a book or its royalties. When presented with computer software, however, many institutional representatives—provosts, legal counsels—will probably claim complete ownership. After all, they'll argue, the institution paid for the time invested in software development; faculty members used *university* computer time.

Suppose a mythical colleague of mine decides to give in and share the royalties. Such a spirit of compromise can lead to more dismay: The university might require the faculty member in question to *reimburse* the college for its expenses *before* claiming any royalty share. Or someone in the sciences, off at the other end of the campus, may suddenly revive the school's patent policy—foreign territory for the English Ph.D., to be sure—leading the university to claim complete ownership of all faculty software products, no matter what the discipline. What's more, the English department software developer suddenly becomes known to the college's legal counsel, who may insist that the university enter into her software publishing contracts—in her place.

Fortunately, major publishers usually won't allow this; they sign authors, not universities. An editor has the weight of an established textbook corporation and its large legal department to throw behind the authors he signs. But what of the murky future? Let's say that I have spent the last four or five years developing various software programs for writing (in fact, I have, but this example is an amalgam of other developers' experiences as well). My software runs daily on the computer laboratory's personal computer network. Who owns the software? Can I take it with me if I leave? Can I leave it behind, secure that someone else won't alter my work after I've gone, particularly if it hasn't been published elsewhere? As of now, experts in computer ethics and software copyright say that I have no guarantees, and possibly no rights. The dilemma might best be resolved through individually tailored, negotiated agreements that protect both faculty and university interests.

Yet there are few precedents to guide those who have been or who will be involved in software projects. Sadly, the few that exist might discourage or completely undermine efforts by humanities faculty members to create good software. Software for writing *must* be developed by writing specialists; unlike textbook preparation, to which it is often (erroneously) compared, software development takes years of writing, revising, testing, implementing, further revising, further testing, and evaluating. It's hard enough to find good software on the market. But what happens to the spirit of a colleague whose software-development interests collide with tangled political issues? Many innovative colleagues will look elsewhere and avoid the software work or implementation research they might otherwise wish to pursue. If political pressure convinces these talented faculty to devote their limited time to a more traditional, narrow sort of "acceptable research," they'll have no other choice. They'll stick to safer, more conservative pursuits, and there will continue to be little acceptable software on the market.

Similarly, I see little rest for faculty who merely wish to acquire commercially available software: Department and university politics often intrude as faculty debate the merits of one type of software over another. Faculty outside the English department—the dean of the business college, for example—may wield the clout to order "Wordstar" for the university computer lab. Consequently, there may not be enough money left in the software budget for the word processing software often preferred by writing faculty—"Applewriter II," "Writing Assistant," or "Word Perfect," for example. Within the department, one forgets the relative youth of the computers-and-writing discipline and the need to try a variety of software products with different purposes and approaches. Just as students' writing needs and purposes vary, so should the eventual contents of university software libraries: Different software programs offer different advantages to writing students at different levels.

Rather than assess a software package's desirability in terms of its demonstration at a major conference, humanities faculty must select good software on the basis of course offerings, varying budgets and constraints, and, most important, students' needs. In fact, proponents of computers within humanities curricula must begin to affirm a place for different *types* of quality software to suit a range of teaching methods, a range that acknowledges student differences. For example, it wasn't until very recently that many specialists began to think critically about well-known major packages. Although the "Writer's Workbench" text-analysis programs from Bell Laboratories are undoubtedly excellent, sophisticated, and useful, the programs deal with only one phase of the writing process. Moreover, the "Workbench" isn't really appropriate for basic writers; it intimidates some students with pages of computer-generated commentary on a 1000-word essay. But some teachers, charged with assessing available software and deciding about purchases, have erroneously assumed that "if other software doesn't do what the 'Workbench' does," it isn't good software.

Note, furthermore, that the issue of software dovetails with the "teacher versus computer" myth, one that strangely and dangerously suggests that one is the same as the other. But computer software is *not* the same as a teacher. First, consider the wide-ranging pedagogical opportunities for implementing different types of software within the curriculum, using the computer to *enhance* the instructor's work, *not to replace* her or it. In a small computer lab with five Apple IIe computers, for example, one instructor divides her class of twenty into two groups. Because computer-group members pair up at a computer, they naturally begin reading to one another the examples demonstrated in the sentence tutorial with which they're working. The noncomputer group begins an essay assignment, perhaps, or receives instruction on writing and punctuation as part of the writing process. When it's time for the two groups to switch, the students who have been at the computer determine how well they've incorporated the computer-aided lesson into their essays by conferring with their peers and the teacher. The same instructor has devised various challenging procedures for free invention and composing during student word processing sessions at the computer. Here, it is the teacher's close work with her students that makes the computer a useful tool—the software itself doesn't perform any miracles.

No matter what the discipline, instructors wouldn't expect one textbook to be the answer for all students at all levels. More often than not, writing instructors leave out chapters of selected texts, supplement the texts they use, and supplement the supplements. My department holds debates on the merits of one textbook over another, basing the arguments on individual teaching styles, preferences, and approaches. Why would a colleague expect anything else of computer-aided instructional programs, given that they're good and well conceived, as he discusses what or what not to purchase?

Many student writers need more than invention and composing strategies; many excellent literature and writing specialists are put off by the word *prewriting* itself and wouldn't consider its inclusion a strong criterion for approving a software package, its central place in recent writing theory and teaching practice notwithstanding. I contend that we should have small libraries of CAI and composing-oriented software to enhance writing and literature instruction; some colleges already have such libraries. But practical considerations, including hardware-compatibility problems and the fairly slow responses of publishers to our software needs—not to mention our usually miniscule budgets—hinder even our most open-minded efforts.

Worse, perhaps, than limited or nonexistent software libraries are administrations that find computing so attractive that they try to replace writing teachers with software. This is another outgrowth of the myth that computers and teachers are interchangeable: A dean at a Midwestern city university, for example, documented a plan to replace composition teachers, particularly at the remedial level (where writers most need one-on-one *teacher*–student interaction) with computer-aided "drill and practice" instruction. And not only administrators subscribe to this myth. At the recent UCLA Conference on Computers and Writing, one colleague, a teacher, happily foresaw a day when computers would free college professors from ever having to teach writing again!

As my earlier example of the computer-equipped writing lab illustrates, those involved in software development or use *must* emphasize this technology's place as an enhancement to expert teaching and research skills. At its best, word processing software offers various advantages that have emerged from recent research into the composing process. For example, as a liberating vehicle for exploratory prewriting and revision, the computer eases the practical problems that discourage student composing and revising (such as making a $20 investment in a typist for a paper's first draft). But I will reiterate what many faculty in writing and other disciplines have learned: Software *itself* doesn't make someone a better writer, chemist, or mathematician. The following sketch illustrates how a good teacher, creatively using software, can do much more than the software can by itself.

> With his freshman composition class in the computer lab that his class shares with other divisions, and with one student seated at each personal computer, Professor X asks the students to spend ten minutes freewriting, nonstop. After this timed exercise (which some students do with the screen's brightness turned down, so they can't see what they're writing and hence worry about the draft's surface features), Professor X asks that they print a hard copy. Then students create a file in which they begin making lists to organize the material they just produced.

There are dozens of variations on this writing instructor's exercise. The software itself is simply a word processor; its use as a device to teach brainstorming and organizing is the teacher's creation. The computer activity, furthermore, is only one part of the instruction. After their computer work, students work with peer revision groups and with the instructor, rethinking and revising (both by hand and by computer) with knowledgeable guidance.

Another, more subtle problem, something I'll call "instructor-centered-ness" (the tendency to assume that "if I like to use this software, then it's good for my students"), can get in the way when one attempts to integrate software into the writing curriculum. In a study I completed with my colleague Tim Redman,[1] we determined that our faculty's successful use of the RUNOFF text-formating program for word processing didn't guarantee our students' successful use of it. Although students were familiar with the program and with the VAX computer system on which it runs, and although they were enthusiastic about writing and revising their papers at the terminal, they found RUNOFF so cumbersome to use that it interrupted their composing processes. The number of revisions they made actually declined when they wrote their papers on the VAX.

Our study raised several important issues, all of which have practical and political implications. Humanities faculty must keep students' needs clearly in mind

[1] "Word-Processing: Expectations versus Experience," *Computers and Composition*, December 1985.

when evaluating or implementing software. And in asserting their authority, instructors must trust themselves, not a colleague elsewhere, to judge how appropriate a particular software program is for their students. For example, while some faculty will be pleased with the business college dean's selection of "Wordstar," others may feel that his selection criteria are not necessarily suitable for humanities applications. Furthermore, although publishers are reluctant to supply trial copies (for copyright and protection reasons), it is productive, when feasible, to allow students to try out potential purchases. In observing a student volunteer, the interested faculty member might discuss the software with him or her, and then judge. Faculty, however, are often trapped by whatever hardware or software the administration happens to have purchased for other disciplines. (Until recently, that was the case with the VAX and word processing at the Illinois Institute of Technology.) The obvious way out of this trap is for writing instructors to be sure they are represented on computer decision-making committees *at the university level*. Such policy-making groups may not only decide which software and hardware to purchase and how much the students will use them but may also determine the *location* of microcomputers and mainframe terminals, a consideration potentially crucial to classroom use.

How have other faculty members at different types of institutions dealt with the politics of CAI and word processing? The introduction of computers into the humanities curriculum has spawned political problems at different levels of academe. A colleague at a small, two-year Texas college notes, "The administration has been supportive—mostly. They have most certainly been allies of the project and devoted to integrating it into the curriculum, providing proper hardware and support, and budgeting money as well as seeking outside funds, respectively."[2] Still, the atmosphere is tense:

> Opposition to the project has come from the technology administration—in the form of brush fires based, I believe, on [the desire to defend] turf and the feeling that English teachers wouldn't know what to do with computers if they had them. This is an archaic bias that crops up too often. I have decided that the real problem is the perception that the more hardware we can have, the less they can have. A second source of irritation has been the learning resources center—recently renamed the library as appropriate—and [staff there] have made waves of obstruction. When the question of space for the lab was considered, the educationists [sic] wanted WWB ["Writer's Workbench"] set up for instruction in the library—and of course, under their domain. It would have been an open lab with no personnel from English to help students—thus it would have been doomed to failure from the start.

This problem can arise even when one collaborates with faculty in other disciplines—an act indispensable to setting up a program of computer use in the humanities. The colleague I've quoted is resolving her problem with a core of loyal administrators and department allies who are helping her fight the "outsiders."

A colleague from a northern college reports similar problems:

[2] The quotes I've used in the text come from material I gathered from colleagues around the country for my book *Computers and Writing: Meeting the Challenge*.

Lest it be thought that the science faculty have handed everything to the humanities on a silver platter, we should note that we have had to argue strenuously for equipment, software, and conditions suitable for writing. Now that so many students use the computer for writing, numbers and demand support our arguments.

Note, however, that this same reasoning (numbers and demand) has served to justify some administrators' decisions to revoke word processing privileges. Computer time, they deem, should be devoted to "more important" concentrations and uses than writing! She continues: "But we pushed for keeping [our access to] a major editor maintained by the computer center (against charges that the humanities people could only understand a simple editor, and that it was their weak minds that made them want such an editor)."

Here, too, the instructor triumphs with a loyal corps of persistent colleagues across the curriculum. But despite her success on one front, she encounters another problem: programmer apathy. Hired to tailor software to the curriculum, the programmers required constant supervision to "make sure they would make changes in software for the sake of learning," changes that seemed essential to her as a writing specialist.

Such programmer-related difficulties stem not only from the usual problems of any collaboration but also from the unarticulated history of divisive perceptions and relationships between humanists and scientists. Although interdisciplinary collaboration often flourishes among faculty, particularly in "writing across the curriculum" efforts, student programmers sometimes cling to the vestiges of an unfortunate myth: that humanistic pursuit is intrinsically less important than scientific investigation. This belief can interfere with their work under humanities faculty members. Moreover, some programmers, student or not, wrongly assume that their supervising faculty person couldn't *possibly* understand the complexities of hardware or software development, despite that faculty member's authority at the university or her knowledge that demonstrates the contrary. In fact, despite warnings about the integrity of the developer's theoretical and pedagogical plan, programmers (typically first- or second-year students in engineering-related disciplines), untrained in composition theory or practice, have assumed the authority to make *substantive* changes in the *text* of software without first consulting the faculty author—an action they are less likely to take when working for physics or mathematics faculty.[3]

[3] Others' anecdotal data underscored by my own, earlier experiences with student programmers. One well-meaning colleague assigned to my project a programmer who was a basic writer (in my class, in fact). His theory was that the student would "learn better" by working for me—not a bad assumption, usually—and that developing tutorial software for writing would improve the programmer's own writing skills. However, bitter that he was placed in my basic writing class to begin with, the student writer/programmer spent most of the semester trying to sabotage work we had already done. I rectified the problem as quickly as I could, not the least because his overzealous programming mischief was taking its toll on his classwork.

Moreover, many student programmers—often a faculty member's only source of programming support—have learned few if any documentation skills. Although one of my programmers, Patrick Woods, has been with me for four years, some student programming help can be short-term. It's difficult, if not impossible, for someone to take over another programmer's half-finished work without clear, decodable records. In short, faculty members often have no choice but to work with programmers who are using them as their training ground. This is valuable experience for all *if* training is part of your purpose.

Other factors enlarge this burgeoning data base of obstructions. A faculty member's needs in any work with computers and writing (or literature, for that matter) may far exceed her or his ability to satisfy them. Such needs raise the specter of conflict in a situation that demands cooperation and collaboration. Here are some typical factors beyond the humanities faculty's control: a lackluster market for commercially available software that leads faculty to try to develop CAI packages of their own; the lack of a sympathetic administration and easily obtainable financial support; an idle computer system that can run UNIX sequestered in the engineering building; student programmers who disappear (or graduate), or forget to document their work for future reference; university policies that haven't yet redefined the concept of valuable work in the humanities. But as more faculty talk and write about the political ramifications of computer work and about their triumphs crossing faculty/administrative boundaries, they can insist not only that it is appropriate for them to have a large part in determining evaluating criteria for hardware and software in their disciplines, but also that determining such criteria is inherent in the nature of faculty positions in the humanities, not adjunct to them. Faculty members need not accept a preordained computer fate any more than would their colleagues with offices or departmental affiliations in computer science.

Our complex mission as professionals involved with or interested in computers and writing, then, includes delivering an important educational message, usually unmentioned in our zeal to develop or implement CAI: No matter how demonstrably significant the long-term results of word processing or computer-aided instructional activities may seem for our students, the student writer and teacher (sometimes joined together as a software development team) are still the most crucial components in understanding and encouraging the writing process. Though strides in computer research over the next few years may give the computer powers that we cannot now imagine, writing and literature specialists will have to decide how to use these new capabilities—and whether to use them *at all*.

For enouragement, I turn to Hugh Burns's recommendation, one of many sage maxims based on his extensive experience. This particular one rings true for humanities computer novices as well as for seasoned developers. Though composition and literature faculty must assert their rights to their own software or look for the best software packages for their students, Burns warns, "Don't make this a lone ranger project in the corner of the department. Set up a software working group across the departments. Trust your best instincts, even if the feedback is negative." And, he declares, work as hard as you can.[4] I'll amplify: Work hard and with help. By contacting individuals with similar interests and problems at other university levels and at other universities, and by making profitable use of those ties, faculty can better prepare to confront the issues a writing specialist with a Ph.D. in literature or rhetoric won't have been trained to expect.

Perhaps I should close this discussion with a formal list of recommendations that could be abstracted, duplicated, and passed along to faculty and administrators. My purpose, however, is to initiate discussion, to raise issues that many in the

---

[4] The direct quote is "Work your buns off." This was written to me in a stream-of-consciousness letter, part of the material I've gathered for *Computers and Writing* from colleagues involved in computer-related work in composition. I'm grateful to them for their insights.

discipline have, for good reason, been reluctant to raise before. So I present no eloquent plea for change but simply a series of requests, some more easily satisfied than others: more faculty voice, more equitable budgets, more equitable hardware and software distribution, more professional recognition and reward for hours upon hours and years upon years of faculty computer work.[5] For we face danger both as teachers and as a society when humanities professionals with computer interests abandon software projects in midstream, fearful of negative tenure decisions or rejection by their colleagues; when, as a result, fewer knowledgeable specialists develop, review, or implement software; and when the humanities *by default* have little or no say about the direction technology will take in the future or about its enlightened use.

---

[5] My work at the Illinois Institute of Technology offers some encouragement: In 1985 I was awarded early tenure at IIT because of (not in spite of) my work with CAI and word processing. Since 1981 I have developed seven tutorials on aspects of the writing process and one prewriting–writing–rewriting "environment" called "The Paragraphing Program," all for the Apple computer. Thanks to the influence of Professors Harold Weinstock (physics) and Henry Knepler (humanities/English), I was encouraged to continue my software development work at the IIT Educational Technology Center, with which I have retained formal ties since becoming Director of Writing Programs at Governors State University. In the fall of 1985, I was working out an agreement on royalties and access to facilities with the IIT administration.

Computers in Thinking, Writing, and Literature

STEPHEN MARCUS

It's not difficult these days to experience a bit of future shock in the face of that familiar and daunting (if somewhat shopworn) adversary: "today's rapidly changing and complex world of technology." It's completely understandable that people would want to withdraw from, or halt, the information overload and the too-rapid shifting of what we English teachers consider the tools of our trade. It's enough to give a person pause, if not a mild-to-severe case of thinker's block.

Before we focus on these new tools of our trade, we might do well to examine such thinking blocks: where they come from, how they affect the kinds of computer-assisted instruction we develop, and how they influence the ways we use, misuse, and fail to use computers in our teaching.

THINKING ABOUT THINKING

The manner in which we use computers to help us think and create depends largely on how we think about thinking. Let's begin with the notion of a "thinking process" that is analogous to the "the composing process."[1] That is, let's propose a working model consisting of **prethinking, thinking, and rethinking**. And before we elaborate, let's remind ourselves that these terms represent recursive stages, not a simple linear progression.

Prethinking includes making the implicit explicit. On a given topic, we generate, record, and note prejudices (ours and those of others). We articulate that which we already possess: facts, memories, feelings, values, and speculations. We might also engage in research to acquire more of this raw material for the thinking process.

The **thinking** stage consists of applying heuristic procedures that use what we've acquired in the prethinking stage. One example would be the activity that Paul Reps describes in *Square Sun, Square Moon*. Children trying to understand the nature of their disagreements are invited to take four perspectives: (1) How are you right and how is the other person wrong? (2) How are you wrong and how is the other person right? (3) How are you both wrong? (4) How are you both right? Such activities help us acquire new kinds of information by assuming new kinds of perspectives. In the present context, "thinking" refers to a special kind of experimentation and discovery.

The **rethinking** stage can be characterized by attaching the prefix *re* to just

[1] This discussion is elaborated in "My Argument With Sheridan: Toward a Thinking Process Model," *South Coast Writing Project Newsletter* 5 (5) (1985).

about any word used to describe mental activity: reconsider, reformulate, reaffirm, and the like. It is in this stage that students can feel free to change their minds—if they think they should—and to articulate those changes.

As in the case of the composing process, some students confuse prethinking with thinking; they mistake affirming and confirming their prejudices with examining them. Others engage in compulsive rethinking. This often leads to thinker's block and is especially troublesome when a paper is due (or when you are trying to decide whether *now* is precisely the best time to buy your first computer).

We can only begin here to explore the utility and limitations of this model of the thinking process. As with a composing process model, this framework's main virtue is that it helps us think about thinking and—if not more important at least more practically—such a framework helps us generate and structure classroom activities that focus on the process, not solely on the product, of students' thinking. For the present, this thinking-process model will help us examine some of the history, the state of the art, and the future of computer-assisted composition and literature instruction.

A THINKING BLOCK

A process model like the one I have described suggests that thinking can become blocked at various stages and for a variety of reasons. For example, attitudes toward the computer's utility in English classes can be described in terms of a kind of arrested development of the prethinking stage. This is part of a historical tradition.

A Series of Thinking Blocks in Reverse Technological Order

The following technologies have been thought by English teachers to lead to the decline of literacy:

- the computer
- television
- movies
- radio
- the typewriter
- the ballpoint pen

It remains to be seen exactly how and to what extent some of these advances will affect students' literacy.[2] The point here, however, is to consider English teachers' attitudes toward these advances in the context of the thinking-process model. In these cases, there were (and are) a variety of influences on the prethinking and rethinking stages. How much these attitudes have resulted from prethinking

---

[2] From a presentation by David Dillon, National Association of Teachers of English, University of Durham, Durham, England, 1984; based on the work of Julie Jensen, *Language Arts*, 60th anniversary issue.

rather than rethinking of facts, fears, and intuitions reflects the somewhat ambivalent relationships that writers and teachers in the humanities have had with technology.

FOUNDATIONS FOR THINKING BLOCKS

English teachers aren't alone, of course, in these problematic times: Their students develop thinking blocks, too. And larger forces than teachers' attitudes shape their students' prethinking about computers—forces that provide vast potential for thinking blocks. School systems and society at large put increasing pressure on students to become computer-literate. Especially where courses in computer use are a required part of the curriculum, more and more students may become computerphobic (just as students have developed math anxiety and blank-page anxiety). Computer literacy courses (courses that teach students basic computer concepts and, possibly, some programming) have become increasingly common: In 1981 only one state mandated computer literacy programs in its public schools; by 1985 eighteen states had laws requiring such efforts.[3]

There is evidence that poor, or just narrowly defined, CAI is already strengthening some teachers' and students' worst thinking blocks—confirming fears about the technology, the people involved in it, and their own capacity to understand it.[4] One only partially prethought notion has it that computers are better suited for males than for females. This can lead to schools giving boys more access to computer labs than they give girls, and even when equal access is granted, the prevalence of software that implicitly supports the prethought "computers for boys" notion makes the lab more attractive to boys than to girls. For example, Hugh Mehan, at the University of California, San Diego, has reported the following:[5]

> Males and females . . . have differential access to computers, especially in secondary schools. In elementary schools that have . . . central computer labs, boys and girls have equal access. However, this equality is not duplicated during voluntary times on computers (recess, lunch, after-school clubs). More boys than girls use computers in their spare time. The equality of access reported in elementary schools disappears in secondary schools. When students are divided into curricular tracks, a stratification of males and females becomes apparent. Males gain greater access to computer . . . labs than females.

Similar prethinking along ethnic and economic lines also leads to inequalities. Mehan further notes that

> Ethnic minority and low-income students receive a different kind of instruction on computers than their middle-income and ethnic majority contemporaries. While middle-income students, especially those who are in advanced programs (e.g., Gifted

[3] *Electronic Learning*, October 1984; "Education Computer News," February 27, 1985.

[4] This discussion is elaborated in "Making the Implicit Explicit: Toward Confluent Computer Literacy," *Teaching, Learning, Computing* 1 (3) (1984).

[5] "The Current State of Computer Use in the Schools," in Report #6, *The Write Help, A Handbook for Computers in Classrooms*, ed. Hugh Mehan and Randall Souviney. (San Diego, Calif.: Center for Human Information Processing, University of California, 1984.)

and Talented Education) receive instruction which encourages learner initiative (programming and problem solving), low-income and ethnic minority students receive instruction which maintains the control of learning within the program (computer-aided drill and practice).

Glenn Fisher, currently at the Lawrence Hall of Science at the University of California, Berkeley, has outlined several specific and interrelated causes for gender bias in CAI, particularly at precollege levels. In general, these are his concerns:[6]

- There is inherent gender bias in software, particularly insofar as educational software has adopted the competitive–aggressive dimensions of arcade games.
- Social stereotypes still identify computers as tools and toys for men and boys.
- Peer pressure and boys' behavior in classrooms still result in boys' being more dominant and intrusive when students are grouped around a computer.
- The content and structure of programming as an introduction to computers still emphasizes math and science examples, exacerbating the gender bias that already exists in those curricular areas.

An extended discussion of these issues isn't possible here. Suffice it to say that gender, race, and socioeconomic status profoundly influence the experience students have with computers before they reach college classrooms, and these experiences establish the foundation of what students (and faculty) think computers are for and *who* they think computers are for. What our students think *about* computers (their prethinking and their patterns of rethinking) and how they think *with* computers are conditioned by their early experiences with computers. We owe it to them, and to ourselves, to broaden our knowledge about computer use in English classes and to rethink carefully our own attitudes about the technology's potential for affecting our curricula.

COMPUTERS AND WRITING: PAST, PRESENT, AND FUTURE

Historically, the development of writing CAI reflects the thinking-process model: It begins with some prethought ideas about how computers can be used for teaching writing, and it progresses through cycles of thinking and rethinking those ideas. This progression can usefully be described in terms of "generations."[7]

The First Generation: Drill and Practice

The first thing one notices about computers is that they are very good at repetition and counting. This observation—part of the prethinking stage—led early developers

---

[6] Presentation at Computer-Using Educators Conference, San Diego State University, San Diego, California, 1983. See also Stephen Marcus, "Sexism and CAI," *Computers, Reading, and Language Arts* 1 (2) (1983).

[7] There are many examples of the kinds of software discussed. This discussion is elaborated, and the names of specific software are given, in Stephen Marcus, "Computers in the Curriculum: Writing," *Electronic Learning* (October 1984). See also Stephen Marcus, "Real-Time Gadgets with Feedback: Special Effects in Computer-Assisted Writing," in *The Computer in Composition Instruction*, ed. Wm. Wresch (Urbana, Ill.: National Council of Teachers of English, 1984).

to produce drill-and-practice programs—programs that present information, test the student's grasp of that information, and repeat the presentation until the student masters the material.

These kinds of programs focus on basic skills such as spelling, punctuation, or sentence combining. Well-designed drill-and-practice software provides instruction that takes advantage of the computer's ability to present information in a compelling and interactive way while keeping track of the students' progress so that it can provide activities that appropriately challenge the students' abilities in needed areas.

First-generation CAI/writing is still used and will undoubtedly continue to improve its capacity for instructing and refining students' basic skills. However, it is with the second-generation software that the computer begins to have a more profound effect on writing.

The Second Generation: Writer Aids

It was soon discovered that, even though drill-and-practice programs taught students the material they were designed to teach, students often didn't carry this knowledge over to their own writing. This discovery probably influenced research into the composing process; in any case, the composing-process model (prewriting, writing, and rewriting as recursive activities) certainly caused CAI developers to rethink their software. Writer aids were the result. This term refers to software that focuses on one or the other stage of the basic composing-process model.

Prewriting software, in general, presents the student with a coherent set of questions modeled on those a teacher might use to elicit the student's own ideas on a topic. The computer–student interaction produces a "dialogue," providing the student with raw material to work into a first draft.

Word processors themselves represent writer aids for the *writing* stage of the composing process. Though not initially designed to *teach* the student anything about writing, word processors—as a new medium—have communicated subtle but profound messages about writing. Students no longer see their words as "carved in stone" but as written in light. Seeing words blink, slide, ripple, disappear, and reappear seems to reinforce the sense that words are more fluid and easily changed and that they represent less of a barrier between having a thought, expressing it, and re-expressing it.

A third kind of writing aid is applicable in the *rewriting* stage. Style and spelling checkers are common examples. More sophisticated revision software provides direct instruction in rethinking early drafts.

It should be noted that second-generation software generally focuses on a single stage of the composing process. The available prewriting aids have virtually no word processing capabilities. Word processors may help you search and replace, but they won't help you figure out what to put there in the first place. Second-generation style and spelling checkers do not provide help with prewriting or word processing.

The Third Generation: Author Systems

Incompatibility of substance, style, and operation between various writer aids limits their usefulness in the classroom: Moving material from a prewriting aid into a word processor file, or using a particular word processor's output with a style checker, for example, can be a difficult and time-consuming task, one that interferes with the very writing process the aids are designed to support. Once developers realized this, they had to do some rethinking. That rethinking led to author systems.

These programs generally provide direct instruction for prewriting, a word processor, and editing and rewriting aids. They have evolved partly from refinements made by people who pioneered the second-generation programs. These systems don't do anything more than the second-generation aids, but they do it all in one package, letting writers move more freely among the various stages of the writing process.

The Fourth Generation: Idea Processors

In certain respects, these kinds of programs could be considered another kind of second-generation prewriting or rewriting aid. But they came somewhat later and have a qualitatively different nature (at least the ones that have more going for them than well-written advertising). They result from another rethinking of how computers can help writers plan their writing. As the name *idea processor* suggests, these programs attempt to help the writer process more than "mere words." They purport to help the writer deal with the relationships between ideas, with their relative value and importance.

The Fifth Generation: Emerging From the "Vaporware"

At this point, fifth-generation writing courseware is a promise ("vaporware") rather than an available product. Fully realized fifth-generation materials will provide increasingly sophisticated author systems. (There are already word processors that alert you to a possible misspelling before you have finished typing the word.) Built-in telecommunications utilities will allow the writer to get prethinking and prewriting information from distant data bases and to obtain reader responses from a wide variety of readers-at-a-distance. Increasingly sophisticated uses of high-resolution graphics will provide writers with the ability to print materials equal in quality to commercially published work. "Multiple windows" and data stored on compact videodiscs will allow a student to read the text of a play in one portion of the screen, watch a performance of the play in another portion of the screen, and write notes for a paper in still another portion.

It should be noted that none of the succeeding generations of CAI/writing software has supplanted previous ones; software representing each generation is currently in use. Teachers and curriculum designers are still thinking and rethinking just how and how much they want to use computers in the writing classroom.

COMPUTERS AND LITERATURE: ATTITUDES

Thinking blocks and prethought attitudes about computers are not, of course, limited to the academic world. Computer technology is pervasive, and even as attitudes toward it harden and polarize, it manages to change the ways in which we think about ourselves and the world.

Pamela McCorduck[8] has discussed extensively our culture's polarized attitudes on the subject of computers and "artificial intelligence": "One [view] says that [computers] are useful, praiseworthy, and appealing; the other . . . says that they are fraudulent, wicked, and even . . . blasphemous."

For many people the construct of artificial intelligence is, in fact, more a reflection of real stupidity.[9]

Sherry Turkle[10] has provided a wonderfully rich perspective on the computer's capacity to evoke such diverse reactions.

> Most considerations of the computer describe it as rational, uniform, constrained by logic. I look at the computer in a different light, not in terms of its nature as an "analytic engine," but in terms of its "second nature" as an evocative object, an object that fascinates, disturbs equanimity, and precipitates thought.

Turkle has explored at some length three stages of young people's concerns with the computer: metaphysics, mastery, and identity. In the first stage, very young children concern themselves with questions about whether a computer is alive. (In paraphrase: "My computer game always beats me. It must be cheating. Only people cheat, so the computer game must somehow be alive.")

Later, students are more concerned with gaining power over the machine, with making it do what they want. In adolescence, their interests shift to questions of self-identity. Adolescents who interact with computers often do their "thinking" about themselves in relation to the machine. Many people used to consider animals as our nearest "relative" on the planet ("Human beings are just animals with rational minds [or with a soul, or that can laugh]"). Now more people are beginning to use the computer as the primary referent. ("We're just computers with emotions.")

The metaphysics–mastery–identity framework is useful for prethinking and rethinking our own attitudes toward technology in general and toward the computer and artificial intelligence in particular. It is also useful as an analytic framework for examining how others have addressed these themes. Consider these diverse works in relation to that framework:

- The Bible (specifically the injunction against graven images)
- *The Iliad* (specifically Hephaestus, who created not only mechanical slaves, but also Pandora)
- *A Connecticut Yankee in King Arthur's Court*
- *Pygmalion*
- *Faust*
- *R.U.R. (Rossman's Universal Robots,* by Karel Capek, the 1923 Czech play that introduced the term "robot")
- *Frankenstein*

[8] *Machines Who Think* (San Francisco: W. H. Freeman, 1979).

[9] I'm indebted for this turn of phrase to Allan November, who appeared on our panel on "Computers in the Curriculum (Part 2)," World Conference on Computers and Education, Norfolk, Virginia, 1985.

[10] *The Second Self: Computers and the Human Spirit.* (New York: Simon and Schuster, 1984).

- *Hard Times*
- *Gulliver's Travels*
- *Brave New World*
- *1984*

Daniel Chandler[11] notes that

> In Britain at least the legacy of literature . . . has been a "civil defense" strategy by English teachers to protect children from the evils of modern industrial society. . . . For such teachers the computer is often just another invasive influence in the classroom. It will no doubt be many years before there is any general shift in this stance.

Computers and Literature: Applications

Attitudes in the United States generally parallel those that Chandler describes. But even though literature serves some as an intellectual defense against computer technology, there are now, for better or worse, numerous applications of computer-assisted instruction in literature. These applications can be roughly categorized as follows:

Tutorials

These relatively interactive programs help students think and write about literature as they lead students through ordered sets of questions. These are usually examples of second-generation writing CAI, though some include rewriting features.[12]

Word Processing Activities

This category refers to word processing files that contain assignments to help students do creative writing or think and write about literature. They do not have the interactive nature of the tutorials, though they can be structured to carry on a dialogue of sorts with the student.[13]

Data Base Courseware

This is a relatively new application of preexisting software (data base managers) to the study of literature. In some cases, the materials provide data bases for study and research purposes.[14] Other such courseware allows students to build their own data bases through thinking and writing activities.[15]

[11] Daniel Chandler and Stephen Marcus, eds. "Computers and Literacy," *Computers and Literacy* (Milton Keynes, England: Open University Press; Philadelphia: Taylor & Francis, 1985).

[12] Examples are SEEN (Helen Schwartz, Department of English, Oakland University, Rochester, Michigan) and GASP (Mark Ferrer, Department of English, University of California, Santa Barbara).

[13] Examples are in Vol. 1: Writing Activities and Language Skill Builders for "The Bank Street Writer" (Scholastic, Inc.); Writing Activities for Scholastic's "PFS:Write" (Scholastic, Inc.), and *Computer Writing Resource Kit* (forthcoming from D. C. Heath).

[14] For example, the Language Arts Files for the Bank Street Filer (Scholastic, Inc.).

[15] For example, the Literature and Composition Activities for Scholastic's PFS: File (Scholastic, Inc.).

Creative Writing Software

This category includes programs that let students create and sometimes illustrate (with computer graphics) traditional as well as interactive stories.[16] Courseware that helps students study and write poetry also falls into this category.[17]

Interactive Fiction

This refers to "stories" in which the particulars of story line and (occasionally) plot and character development result from the choices the "reader" (who is in some sense also the writer) makes in the course of using the software.[18]

Computer-assisted instruction for literature has not progressed through the various generations that writing software has; most of its development has not gotten very far beyond the prethinking stage. What applications do exist have begun to encourage people to rethink the relationship between computers and the study or creation of literature.

WHAT? SO WHAT? NOW WHAT?

Up to this point, we have encountered a complex collection of topics, concepts, categories, and crosscurrents. As they converge, they determine the nature of our students, the nature of the instructional tools available to us, and the nature of our enterprise as teachers of reading, thinking, and writing.

What real difference will this all make for us and our students tomorrow? Next semester? Next year?

Some people are doing what they can to ensure that very little will happen. With ungovernable and uncertain transitions (our "rapidly changing and complex world") comes a predictable kind of retrenching. The editors of *Educational Technology* have already noted (August 1984) that "it has taken longer than usual for the critics to begin to pummel this particular innovation in the schools, but now the backlash against computers in education has begun."

We can certainly all stand to rethink our attitudes about the uses of technology in our work, and we should constantly reassess the promise and problems of specific computer applications in the teaching of writing and in the study of literature. We should also engage in more prethinking, in making more explicit what we need to know and what we don't want to know about computers and the teaching of English.

---

[16] Examples include "Story Tree" (Scholastic, Inc.), "Story Maker" (D. C. Heath), and The Bank Street Story Book (Mindscape).

[17] For example, Compupoem (Stephen Marcus, South Coast Writing Project, University of California, Santa Barbara).

[18] For example, *Hitchhiker's Guide to the Galaxy* (Infocom); *Robots of Dawn* (Epyx); *Swiss Family Robinson, Wizard of Oz, Treasure Island, Wind in the Willows, Alice in Wonderland* (Windham Classics), and *Fahrenheit 451* (Trillium).

> # One Final Thinking Block
>
> When asked about the computer, many English teachers would express an attitude similar to this:
>
> > [It] destroys memory [and] weakens the mind, relieving it of . . . work that makes it strong. [It] is an inhuman thing.

As many readers know, this remark was not made about the computer. It is to be found in Plato, and the reference is to writing.[19] The future of literacy (that is, the nature and proficiency of reading, thinking, and writing skills) is as problematic now as it has been in the past—particularly so in the context of an educational medium that is as often considered a distrusted intruder as it is taken to be a helpful ally.

If anything can be predicted about computers and literacy,[20] it is that some people will oversell the technology as a positive force and that others will decry it as an abomination. Perhaps the most we can hope for is a continued reliance on talented teachers who acquire an informed exuberance. As always, it is their prethinking, thinking, and rethinking that will be a major force in making the most of whatever the technology—and their students—have to offer.

---

[19] From an address by Hans Ruttiman to the International Conference on Computers and the Humanities, Raleigh, North Carolina, 1983.

[20] For a list of predictions, see Stephen Marcus, "The Future of Literacy," in *Computers and Literacy*, ed. Daniel Chandler and Stephen Marcus (Milton Keynes, England: Open University Press; Philadelphia: Taylor & Francis, 1985).

BIBLIOGRAPHY

Appleby, Bruce C. "Computers and Composition: An Overview." *Focus* 9 (Spring 1983).

Arms, Valarie M. "The Computer as an Aid to Collaborative Writing." *The Technical Writing Teacher.* XI (Spring 1984), 181–185.

———. "Creating and Recreating." *College Composition and Communication* 34 (October 1983): 355–358.

———. "A Dyslexic Can Compose on a Computer." *Educational Technology* 24 (January 1984): 39–41.

Balkema, Sandra J. "Studying the Composing Activities of Experienced Computer Writers." In *Computers and Composition: Proceedings of the Conference on Computers in Writing: New Directions in Teaching and Research,* edited by Lillian S. Bridwell and Donald Ross. Houghton, Mich.: Michigan Technological University, 1984, pp. 23–35.

Bates, Peter. "How to Turn Your Writing into Communication." *Personal Computing* October 1984: 84–93.

Bean, J. "Computerized Word-Processing as an Aid to Revision." *College Composition and Communication* 34 (May 1983): 146–148.

Bonner, Paul. "Enter, the Powerful New Idea Tools." *Personal Computing,* January 1984.

Booth, Wayne C. "Catching the Overflow." *College English* 46 (February 1984): 140–142.

Bourque, J. "Understanding and Evaluating: The Humanist as a Computer Specialist." *College English* 45 (January 1983).

Bridwell, Lillian S., Parker Johnson, and Stephen Brehe. "Composing and Computers: Case Studies of Experienced Writers." In *Writing in Real Time: Modelling Production Processes,* edited by Ann Matsuhashi. Norwood, N.J.: Ablex, in press.

Bridwell, Lillian S., Donald Ross, and Paula Reed Nancarrow. "The Writing Process and the Writing Machine: Current Research on Word Processors Relevant to the Teaching of Composition." In *New Directions in Composition Research,* edited by Richard Beach and Lillian S. Bridwell. New York: Guilford Press, 1984.

Bridwell, Lillian S., Geoffrey Sirc, and Robert Brooke. "Revising and Computing: Case Studies of Student Writers." In *The Acquisition of Written Language: Revision and Response,* edited by Sarah Friedman. Norwood, N.J.: Ablex, in press.

Brohaugh, William. "The Hazards of Electronic Writing." *Popular Computing* April 1984: 126–131.

Burns, Hugh. "Stimulating Rhetorical Invention in English Composition through Computer-Assisted Instruction," *ERIC Document 188 245* (1979).

Case, Donald P. "Processing Professorial Words: Personal Computers and the Writing Habits of University Professors." *College Composition and Communication* 36 (October 1985): 317–322.

Catano, James V. "Computer-Based Writing: Navigating the Fluid Text." *College Composition and Communication* 36 (October 1985): 309–316.

Chandler, Daniel, and Stephen Marcus, eds. *Computers and Literacy.* Milton Keynes, England: Open University Press; Philadelphia: Taylor & Francis, 1985.

Clark, Gary. *Computers and Young Minds*. Chatsworth, Calif.: Datamost, 1984. Reprinted in *The Computing Teacher*, 12 (May 1985): 8–9.

Coleman, Eve B. "Flowcharting as a Prewriting Activity." *Computers, Reading and Language Arts* 1 (Winter 1983): 36–38.

Collier, Richard M. "The Word Processor and Revision Strategies." *College Composition and Communication* 34 (May 1983): 149–155.

———. "Writing and the Word Processor: How Wary of the Gift-Giver Should We Be?" In *Computers and Composition: Selected Papers from the Conference on Computers in Writing: New Directions in Teaching and Research*. Special issue. Edited by Lillian Bridwell and Donald Ross. Houghton, Mich.: Michigan Technological University, 1985, pp. 67–93.

Daiute, Colette. "The Computer as Stylus and Audience." *College Composition and Communication* 34 (May 1983): 134–145.

———. *Writing and Computers*. Reading, Mass.: Addison-Wesley, 1985.

Dreyfus, Hubert L. *What Computers Can't Do: The Limits of Artificial Intelligence*. New York: Harper & Row, 1979.

Elias, R. "Will Computers Liberate the Comp Drudge?" *ERIC Document 241 954* (1984).

Etchison, Craig. "Who's Making the Decisions—People or Machines?" *Computers and Composition* 2 (August 1985): 17–26.

Feigenbaum, Edward A., and Pamela McCorduck. *The Fifth Generation: Artificial Intelligence and Japan's Computer Challenge to the World*. New York: New American Library, 1984.

Gerrard, Lisa. "From Wylbur to WANDAH: Designing Software for Student Writers." In *Computers and Composition: Proceedings of the Conference on Computers in Writing: New Directions in Teaching and Research*, edited by Lillian S. Bridwell and Donald Ross. Houghton, Mich.: Michigan Technological University, 1984, pp. 125–138.

———. "Using a Computerized Text Editor in Freshman Composition." *ERIC Document 227 512* (1983).

———. "Writing with Wylbur: Teaching Freshman Composition with a Mainframe Computer." *ERIC Document 239 299* (1984).

Green, J. O. "Computers, Kids, and Writing: An Interview with Donald Graves." *Classroom Computer Learning* 4 (1984): 20–22, 28.

Halpern, Jeanne W., and Sarah Liggett. *Computers and Composing: How the New Technologies Are Changing Writing*. Carbondale, Ill.: Southern Illinois University Press, 1984.

Harris, Jeanette. "Student Writers and Word Processing: A Preliminary Evaluation." *College Composition and Communication* 36 (October 1985): 323–330.

Haselkorn, Mark P., and Robert J. Connors. "Computer Analysis of the Composing Process." In *Computers and Composition: Proceedings of the Conference on Computers in Writing: New Directions in Teaching and Research*, edited by Lillian S. Bridwell and Donald Ross. Houghton, Mich.: Michigan Technological University, 1984, pp. 139–158.

Holdstein, Deborah H. "Word-Processing: Expectations versus Experience." *Computers and Composition*, forthcoming.

Kiefer, Kate, and Charles Smith. "Textual Analysis with Computers: Tests of Bell Laboratories' Computer Software." *Research in the Teaching of English* 17 (October 1983): 201–214.

Kolata, Gina. "Equal Time for Women." *Discover* 5 (January 1984): 24–27.

Lees, Elaine O. "Proofreading with the Ears: A Case Study of Text-to-Voice Performance of a Student's Writing." In *Collected Essays on the Written Word and the Word Processor*, edited by Thomas E. Martinez. Villanova, Penna.: Villanova University, 1984, pp. 218–230. Reprint in *Collegiate Microcomputer*, forthcoming.

Marcus, Stephen. "Hal to Pal?" *Computers, Reading and Language Arts* 1 (Winter 1983): 8, 33.

———. " Sexism and CAI." *Computers, Reading and Language Arts* 1 (Fall 1983).

———. "Real-Time Gadgets with Feedback: Special Effects in Computer-Assisted Writing." *The Writing Instructor* 2 (Summer 1983): 156–164.

Marcus, Stephen, and Sheridan Blau. "Not Seeing Is Relieving: Invisible Writing with Computers." *Educational Technology* 23 (April 1983): 12–15.

Marling, William. "Grading Essays on a Microcomputer." *College English* 46 (December 1984): 797–810.

McCorduck, Pamela. *Machines Who Think*. New York: W. H. Freeman, 1980.

McDaniel, Ellen. "A Bibliography of Text-Analysis and Writing-Instruction Software." *Journal of Advanced Composition*, forthcoming.

Nancarrow, Paula Reed, Donald Ross, and Lillian Bridwell, eds. *Word Processors and the Writing Process: An Annotated Bibliography*. Westport, Conn.: Greenwood Press, 1985.

Nold, Ellen. "Fear and Trembling: The Humanist Approaches the Computer." *College Composition and Communication* 26 (1975): 269–273.

Ohmann, Richard. "Literacy, Technology and Monopoly Capital." *College English* 47 (November 1985): 675–689.

Papert, Seymour. *MindStorms*. New York: Basic Books, 1980.

Paul, Terri, and Don Payne. "Computer-Assisted Instruction: Teaching and Learning from Basic Writers." *The Writing Instructor* 2 (Summer 1983): 193–199.

Peterson, Ivars. "Bits of Ownership." *Science News*. 21 September, 1985: 188–190.

Piper, Karen L. "Separating Wheat from Chaff: Evaluating Word Processing Programs for Language Arts Instruction." *Computers, Reading and Language Arts* 1 (Winter 1983): 9–11.

Reps, Paul. *Square Sun, Square Moon: A Collection of Prose Essays*. Rutland, Vt.: Tuttle, 1967.

Rodrigues, Dawn. "Computers and Basic Writers." *College Composition and Communication* 36 (October 1985): 336–339.

Rodrigues, Raymond J., and Dawn Wilson. "Computer-Based Invention: Its Place and Potential." *Composition and Communication* 35 (February 1984): 78–87.

Russ-Eft, Darlene F., Donald H. McLaughlin, and Annalee Elman. *Issues for the Development of Reading and Writing Software*. Palo Alto, Calif.: American Institute for Research in the Behavioral Sciences, 1983.

Schank, Roger C., with Peter G. Childers. *The Cognitive Computer: On Language, Learning, and Artificial Intelligence*. Reading, Mass.: Addison-Wesley, 1985.

Schwartz, Helen. "The Confessions of Professor Strangelove; Or, An Apology for Literacy." *Computers and Composition* 1 (August 1985): 6–16.

———. "Monsters and Mentors: Computer Applications for Humanistic Education." *College English* 44 (February 1982).

———. "Teaching Writing with Computer Aids." *College English* 46 (March 1984): 239–247.

Schwartz, Helen, and Lillian S. Bridwell. "A Selected Bibliography on Computers in Composition." *College Composition and Communication* 34 (February 1984).

Selfe, Cynthia, and Billie Wahlstrom. "The Benevolent Beast: Computer-Assisted Instruction for Teaching Writing." *The Writing Instructor* 2 (Summer 1983).

Smith, John B., and Catherine F. Smith. "Spatial Thinking and Top-Down Writing." In *Computers and Composition: Proceedings of the Conference on Computers in Writing:*

New Directions in Teaching and Research, edited by Lillian S. Bridwell and Donald Ross. Houghton, Mich.: Michigan Technological University, 1984, 257–270.

Sommers, Elizabeth A., and James L. Collins, eds. *Writing On-Line: Using Computers in the Teaching of Writing.* Upper Montclair, N.J.: Boynton/Cook, 1985.

————. "Microcomputers and Writing." *Computers and Composition* 2 (August 1984): 27–35.

Southwell, Michael G. "Computer Assistance for Teaching Writing: A Review of Existing Programs." *Collegiate Microcomputer* 2 (August 1984): 193–206.

————. "Computer-Assisted Instruction in Composition at York College/CUNY: Grammar for Basic Writing Students." *The Writing Instructor* 2 (Summer 1983): 165–173.

Sudol, Ronald A. "Applied Word Processing: Notes on Authority, Responsibility, and Revision in a Workshop Model." *College Composition and Communication* 36 (October 1985): 331–335.

Turkle, Sherry. *The Second Self: Computers and the Human Spirit.* New York: Simon and Schuster, 1984.

Waldrop, M. Mitchell. "Machinations of Thought." *Science 85* (March 1985): 38–45.

————. "Natural Language Understanding." *Science* 224 (April 27, 1984): 372–374.

Weizenbaum, Joseph. *Computer Power and Human Reason.* San Francisco: W.H. Freeman, 1976.

Winograd, Terry. "Computer Software for Working with Language." *Scientific American* (September 1984): 131–145.

Wresch, William, ed. *The Computer in Composition Instruction: A Writer's Tool.* Urbana, Ill.: National Council of Teachers of English, 1984.

Zimmerman, Jan, ed. *The Technological Woman: Interfacing with Tomorrow.* New York: Praeger, 1983.

ABOUT THE CONTRIBUTORS

Valarie Meliotes Arms is an assistant professor in the Department of Humanities and Communications at Drexel University. The designer of several software programs, she serves as computer consultant to several colleges and is editor of *IEEE Transactions on Professional Communications*. Arms has published on computing, composition, and the work of William Styron and other modern writers. Her extensive publication list includes reviews and articles in numerous journals, including *College Composition and Communication, Technical Communication, Collegiate Microcomputer, Contemporary Literature,* and *Journal of Modern Literature.*

Diane P. Balestri is assistant dean of the College, Princeton University. Educated at Wellesley and Yale, she has taught at Southern Connecticut State, Connecticut, Albertus Magnus, and Bryn Mawr. At Bryn Mawr she was also associate dean and director of the Summer Institute for Women in Higher Education Administration. Currently, Balestri chairs the FIPSE Technology Study Group, made up of 70 FIPSE-funded educatiors who are collaborating via teleconferencing to produce a book about computers in higher education. In addition, she has been a consultant to the Exxon Foundation and the Annenberg/CPB Project.

Michael E. Cohen serves as UCLA Writing Programs's Software and Media Consultant and was principal programmer for the Word Processor Writing Project, which produced WANDAH (now *HBJ Writer*). He is the author of the HOMER text analysis program and IMITATIO Suite, a series of programs for producing concordances and performing other tasks for literary scholars. At the Jet Propulsion Laboratory's Deep-Space Network, he composed systems performance test software. Cohen holds a UCLA degree in motion picture and television production. In his spare time, he writes science fiction.

David N. Dobrin is president of Organizational Communications Consultants in Cambridge, Massachusetts, where he collaborated on the design of the documentation system for a fifth-generation text editor. After earning his Ph.D. at the University of California, San Diego, Dobrin taught in California, Ohio, and Massachusetts. He is the author of a book, *Straightforward Writing: Writing in a Technological Society,* and of articles published in *College English, IEEE Transactions in Professional Communications, The Technical Writing Instructor,* and several anthologies. His current research concerns product liability law.

Lisa Gerrard is on the faculty of the UCLA Writing Programs, where she was design consultant on the WANDAH (*HBJ Writer*) project, and is the author of *Writing With HBJ Writer: A Rhetoric for Computer-Assisted Composition*. She received her Ph.D. from the University of California, Berkeley, and has published and presented papers about nineteenth-century fiction and women's studies as well as computers and composition. In addition to teaching basic, freshman, and advanced composition, she teaches courses in business and legal writing and in writing pedagogy for Spanish language instruction.

Andrea W. Herrmann, an assistant professor of English at the University of Arkansas at Little Rock, earned her Ed.D. from Teachers College, Columbia University, in 1985. The article in this volume grew out of two years of qualitative research that culminated in her dissertation, "Using the Computer as a Writing Tool: Ethnography of a High School Writing Class." She has conducted workshops and published articles on topics related to education, TESOL, composition, and computers. Herrmann is currently writing a book, *Teaching Writing with Computers: K–12*.

Deborah H. Holdstein is director of Writing Programs at Governors State University in Illinois, where she develops and teaches courses in rhetoric, computers, composition, and pedagogy. An Illinois Ph.D., Holdstein has composed a variety of software packages, has published widely, and is the author of a forthcoming book, *Computers and Writing: Ways of Meeting the Challenge*. She is also a member of the Executive Committee of the Conference on College Composition and Communication. Her research interests include writing across the curriculum, business and professional writers' revision processes, and remediation needs of returning students, particularly women.

Edward M. Jennings is a member of the English faculty at SUNY at Albany, where he teaches nonfiction writing, technology and writing, practical writing, science fiction, and the British novel. A Wisconsin Ph.D., Jennings has published in *College Composition and Communication, Studies on Voltaire, The Eighteenth Century*, and *The Dune Encyclopedia*. He originated NEMLA's computer division and compiled *Science and Literature* (1970). He is interested in the intersections of semiotic, cognition, artificial-intelligence, creativity, composition, information, and general systems theories.

Erna Kelly teaches technical writing, composition, women's studies, and seventeenth-century literature at the University of Wisconsin—Eau Claire, where she is an assistant professor of English. After receiving her Ph.D. at SUNY at Albany, she taught at Russell Sage and UCLA. Kelly has published and presented papers about Lovelace, Whitman, Wordsworth, humor, and the psycholinguistics of gender; she has also edited a book of cross-curricular readings for advanced writing. Her research interests are the composing process, Cavalier poetry, and images of women in Renaissance literature.

Elaine O. Lees was formerly director of the Basic Writing Program and coordinator of the College of General Studies Composition Program at the University of Pittsburgh, where she earned her Ph.D. in 1976. In addition to her work with computers and writing, she has published articles on pedagogy, editing, and the perception of error. Her research interests also include the relationships between critical theory and the teaching of writing. At present, Lees does educational consulting in the Pittsburgh area and teaches composition part-time at Carnegie-Mellon University.

Stephen Marcus is associate director of the South Coast Writing Project, Graduate School of Education, University of California, Santa Barbara. His publications include *Computers and Literacy* (with Daniel Chandler), *Computer Writing Resource Kit*, and *Compupoem*, which was named in a national survey of teachers' favorite software. Marcus serves on statewide, national, and international boards, including a United Kingdom advisory committee for establishing guidelines for computer use in English instruction.

Don Payne teaches at Iowa State University, where he is an associate professor of English. His courses include rhetoric, business and technical writing, pedagogy, and composition theory; he has published articles on computer-assisted instruction, principles of courseware design, and speaking–writing relationships. Currently Payne is researching problem-solving strategies for basic writers, conceptual frameworks for rhetorical analysis, and the rhetoric of scientists' and humanists' debates about computers. He likes to imagine Mark Twain's response to computing: "All the modern inconveniences" (*Life on the Mississippi*).

John E. Thiesmeyer is an associate professor at Hobart and William Smith Colleges. A teacher of literature and composition for over twenty years, he completed doctoral work in British nineteenth-century literature and was assistant editor of the computer concordance to Blake's writings published by Cornell in 1967. He began investigating other educational uses of computers in 1981 and is co-developer of *Editor*, a microcomputer text-analysis system that can identify over 10,000 problems in usage and mechanics. The subjects of his publications include Hopkins, linguistics and prosodic theory, and computer-assisted writing instruction.

John C. Thoms received his B.A. in English and Greek from Swarthmore College and his Ph.D. in medieval English literature from Columbia University. He is now an associate professor of English at the New York Institute of Technology, where he teaches basic writing and reading, technical and business writing, and a variety of literature courses. Besides developing, and training faculty for, the computer-assisted course described in his essay, he has designed and written three software programs for use with the Commodore-64 microcomputer: the *LogiComp* exercises in levels of generalization, a vocabulary development program, and (with his wife, Judith J. Thoms) an on-line introduction to the PaperClip word processor. Since 1984 he has spoken frequently at conferences on computers and writing. His current research interests include the educational uses of computer conferencing.

Ruth Chervin Von Blum is director of biology course development for Wasatch Education Systems in Salt Lake City. She earned her Ph.D. in Science and Mathematics Education from the University of California, Berkeley, where she served on the faculty for five years. She was director of UCLA's Word Processor Writing Project, which developed WANDAH (*HBJ Writer*), and has had major writing, research, development, and consultation responsibilities for a number of grants. Von Blum has given presentations and published articles and reviews on such topics as computer-assisted learning, computers and writing, biology education, and scientific reasoning. She is the author of the book *Mendelian Genetics: A Problem-Solving Approach.*